Why does it make **GOOD SENSE** to   See Page

    Put candles in the freezer?   70
    Dab butter on a pitcher spout?   98
    Put marbles in a double boiler?   68
    Keep drinking straws in your jewel box?   61

When does it make **GOOD SENSE** to

    Put socks on your hands?   87
    Drive your car over a carpet?   74
    Wash your hands with peanut butter?   56
    Put rubber bands around a drinking glass?   34

GOOD SENSE is good news for anyone who's ever
cooked a meal, sewn a dress, raised children, plants or
animals, driven a car, done a wash. It's for everyone
who's ever wondered how to cut a *raw* egg in half, dry
dishes *without* a towel, get the salt *out* of the soup.
You'll save pennies, kilowatts, stitches, tears, inches,
minutes, calories, footsteps, ounces, by using your

GOOD SENSE

GOOD SENSE

by Betty Bergman Levin with Charlotte King

ZEBRA BOOKS

KENSINGTON PUBLISHING CORP.

ZEBRA BOOKS
are published by
KENSINGTON PUBLISHING CORP.
521 Fifth Avenue
New York, N.Y. 10017

The following don't need any hints to know
why we couldn't have done it without them.
Lewis Barlow
Robert M. Bennett
Molly P. Bergman
Emily J. Buchbinder
Susan P. Buchbinder
Santina R. Curran
Barbara B. O'Brien
Paul Rich

and a very special thanks to
Janet Langhart and John Willis, Hosts,
Bruce R. Marson, Producer,
all the staff and the crew of
"Good Morning!"
and its viewers on the
New England Network
whose ideas greatly inspired this book.

Special thanks to Richard Dickinson for the
research and selection of graphics.

illustrations by MONA PALM

First Printing: August, 1977
Printed in the United States of America

CONTENTS: A BAKER'S DOZEN

Chapter 1
MOTHER EARTH'S OFFSPRING
tending to plants and animals   9

Chapter 2
KIDS ARE NOT BABY GOATS
more joy from parenting   24

Chapter 3
DOMESTIC TRANQUILLITY
protection and care of person and property   44

Chapter 4
FUEL-PROOF
energy-savers and energy-users   63

Chapter 5
A CLEAN SWEEP
the challenge of daily chores   80

Chapter 6
DISH-ORGANIZED
kitchen short-cuts   96

Chapter 7
FOOD FARE
ways to prepare   107

Chapter 8
CONSERVE AND PRESERVE
extending the versatility of food   127

Chapter 9
A SECOND LOOK
home renewal and recycling   140

Chapter 10
STITCH-N-TIME
sewing and other needle arts   157

Chapter 11
GRIN AND WEAR IT
the care of clothing and fabrics   169

Chapter 12
GETTING IT ALL TOGETHER
think-ahead thoughts   187

Chapter 13
THE LIVING END
an offbeat assortment of ideas   200

Each generation's lifestyle reflects the conditions and the concerns of the times. And to maintain this lifestyle each family has developed its own secret formulas for tackling simple chores and attacking challenging projects.

Thanks to the ecology movement, the energy crisis, commodity shortages and the general economic condition, many people are returning with relief and pride to the ways of earlier generations. Indeed, great-grandma would be right at home today. Somehow Grandma Glady's secrets for stretching sugar, Uncle Uriah's guidelines for growing gardens and Aunt Agatha's methods for eliminating obnoxious odors seem to hold up just fine!

The present generation has also been creative and has expanded, updated and virtually recycled many old chestnuts into new workable solutions for contemporary living. While recycling, rehabilitating, stretching and saving isn't everyone's missionary cause, there is no doubt that it has become both serious and chic.

Within these pages is a collection of nearly a thousand shared secrets. By and large they are homemade, homespun and home-tested. In addition to their intrinsic practical value, they should serve as thought-starters — an impetus towards finding your own solutions for everyday-living situations. We hope that you will fill the margins of the book and the pages at the back with your own ingenuous formulas so that your ideas along with those you find here—will be passed on to future folks!

We will consider our task accomplished if you discover that—in doing things better, faster, cheaper and simpler—genuine warmth and good humor do mix well with GOOD SENSE.

Chapter 1
MOTHER EARTH'S OFFSPRING
tending to plants and animals

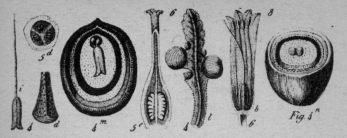

Use plastic gallon containers as hot caps to protect delicate tomato or other plants. Cut off the bottom half and use the top half to cover the plants. Be sure to unscrew the top.

To start plants in the house, use eggshell halves filled with loam. Place shells in the twelve compartments of an egg carton. When the plants are established, transplant them right in the shells. The roots will break through as the egg shells decompose.

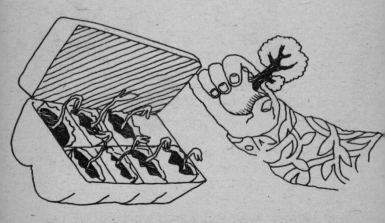

Enrich your garden organically by using the old American Indian technique of burying fish in the garden soil. It adds nutrients and minerals to the soil and stimulates the growth of beneficial microbes. To keep dogs and cats away, sprinkle wood ashes over the fish and then cover with a layer of soil.

Sow small seeds such as carrots and radishes by placing them in empty spice jars with shaker tops. Shake out seeds and cover the rows to prevent the wind from blowing away the seeds. Result: more rows per package; less thinning necessary.

Lay a strip of old tissue paper on the table and with a tweezer place the seeds the prescribed distance apart. Use an eye dropper to place a drop of clear, dissolved gelatin over each seed, thereby securing it to the tissue.

A few moth crystals around outdoor bushes and plants will repel bugs. No need for dangerous pesticides.

Mothballs placed around the plants in your garden will keep animals from nibbling at them or destroying them.

Pretty insect and animal repellents can be found in the plant kingdom itself. Nasturtium and herbs, planted among vegetables in a

garden, keep insects and small animals away.
And you'll have flowers for your home and
herbs for your cooking.

Spray your vegetables with a pint of water in
which you have crushed two or three cloves
of garlic. The odor will repel animals who
otherwise might eat the vegetables in your
garden.

Fireplace ashes can be put into service in the
summer. Sprinkle the ashes around the base
of the plants to keep them healthy and
stimulate their growth.

About two to three hours before weeding
your garden, water it. This will loosen the
soil, make the weeding easier and result in less
damage to surrounding plants.

When planting seeds indoors, make a
greenhouse out of heavy, transparent plastic.
You'll have optimum conditions for raising
seedlings and plants.

Tie tomato plants to a stake with cut up
strip of pantyhose. The nylon is soft but
strong and stretches. It also acts as an
electrical conductor which is beneficial for
the plants.

Formula for perennial pleasure: when the
blossoms begin to drop from a forced branch
of forsythia and the green leaves appear,
transfer the branch to another container filled
with warm water to stimulate root growth.
When the weather is warm outside, plant in
the ground in full sun and next spring "Enjoy."

To dry homegrown onions, loosen the soil around them with a fork. Leave the tops on; just pin them on a line by their tops with clothespins. Air-dry for a couple of weeks.

When already picked onions begin to sprout, plant them in a pot as you would any plant. Within a week or two, the green tips can be cut and used as you would chives. They have a mild onion flavor.

A handy measuring tool for the garden is the stick on your hoe. Paint stripes on it to indicate 1, 2, 3 foot lengths and you won't have to guess distances when planting.

Garden tools won't rust if after use you run them through a box filled with a mixture of 1/3 sand and 2/3 motor oil.

Use an old hibachi as a planter either indoors or outdoors. Clean off the metal and wood parts and paint with a rust retardant. Fill the bottom with stones or gravel and place potting or prepared soil above. Makes a handsome plant container.

Sterile soil is the best medium for potting plants. You can do it yourself (if you can tolerate the unpleasant odor!) by putting soil in a large roaster or baking pan. Add enough water to moisten and bake at 180 degrees 30 minutes in a tightly covered pan.

Encourage your window plants to grow in more than one direction. Cut a piece of mirror the size of your window sill. Place your plants on it. The sun, reflecting in the mirror, produces rays of sunshine all over the plant.

Foam plastic drinking cups with holes punched in the bottom can be decorated and used as small planters. Supermarket meat trays placed under them can serve as the saucers to catch the excess moisture.

Punch holes in the top of discarded plastic caps from spray cans and use as a pot for a seedling. The range of colors allows you to coordinate them so you know which seedling is in which pot.

To insure proper drainage for your house plants, place a fluted-edge cap from soft drinks or beer bottles over the hole at the bottom of the pot before planting. The fluting allows the water to drain, but the cap retains the soil.

Slip a plastic bowl cover or shower cap over the bottom of the pot before watering a hanging plant. It will catch drips and save the flooring.

Use a meat baster to water African violets. You will avoid getting water on the leaves.

COFFEE, TEA OR MILK. . .

R$_x$ for sick plants: Put several crushed egg shells into an empty plastic bottle filled with water. Let stand for a few days and use to water ailing plants. The mixture can also be used as lime on outdoor plants.

Treat your plants to a healthy shine. Recipe for plant polish:

1) Place used tea bags and egg shells in a clean plastic gallon jug.
2) Completely cover with water
3) Mix 1/3 of this mixture with 2/3 of water every couple of weeks and put on plants.

You'll have shiny, healthy looking plants.

Ferns and other plants thrive on tea.
Pour any leftover tea on your plants.

Before discarding empty milk cartons, fill with water and save for watering plants. Leftover or soured milk mixed with water adds shine to your plants. Truly good to the last drop!

Club soda that has gone flat is good for watering plants. The chemicals which remain add vigor and color to your greenery.

No need to have someone house-sit for your plants! To keep plants watered while away, push a needle threaded with wool into the soil of your plant pot and put the other end of the wool into a jar of water. The soil will stay moist for weeks.

or

Place plant pots on bath towels in the bathtub and water from the top. Towels will hold enough moisture for up to three weeks. Keep drain open so excess water can drain from the bathtub.

BEAUTIFUL BLOSSOMS

To transport home-cut flowers without messy buckets of water, fill some small balloons with water. Put the stem into the balloon and secure with a rubber band.

If your cut flowers are too short for your tall vase, tape the end of the stem to a straw. Fill with enough water to cover the end of the stem.

Preserve the freshness of cut flowers. If you dip their stems in hot water, they will expand and absorb more moisture.

Add one tablespoon of sugar to the water in your vase to extend the life of cut flowers.

A few drops of oil of cloves added to the water in the vase will also prolong the life and loveliness of your bouquet.

To freshen water for floral arrangements without disturbing the flowers, use a turkey baster to remove and replenish the water.

Color white flowers by using food coloring as water in the vase. Blue daisies, green carnations—use your imagination to suit your mood and color scheme.

To preserve a special bouquet of flowers, spray them with hair spray about five times. Let dry between sprays. Five applications in one day will preserve your bouquet for several years. You can keep your memories intact.

FELINE FINE

To keep a kitty box smelling fresh, put a pine-scented cleaner, which kills bacteria, in the bottom. Let dry before adding the kitty litter.

Another way to keep kitty's box fresh smelling is by sprinkling the pan with baking soda!

If your cat eats your plants, place some grain or catnip in a flower pot and put it near your cat's favorite plant. The cat will devour the treat rather than your plant.

Hair spray will repel cats. So give your artificial flowers a spray and they won't be used as feline food.

It's safer to use a harness which goes around the chest as well as the neck than to put only a collar on a cat. However, a carrying case is the safest method for transporting a cat. Second choice is a harness with a leash.

To feed a cat liquid medicine, spill some on the fur and your instinctively clean cat will lick it off instantly.

CANINE CARE

Keep dog bones in your freezer. They stay
fresh that way and you always have one on
hand. Dogs don't seem to mind frozen bones.

Instead of washing your dog's coat, brush out the dirt every day with baby powder or baking soda. It rids the coat of dirt and leaves your dog smelling good.

or

Just vacuum your dog! Your pet's easier to vacuum than your home. The dog may resist at first, but some dogs do learn to enjoy it.

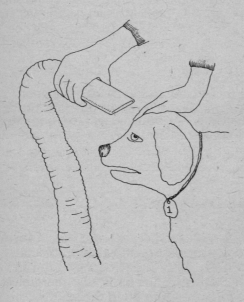

A good anti-bacterial soap works just as effectively on a dog and is cheaper than dog shampoo.

If you put butter on a pill, a dog will eat it like candy.

Glue a rubber fruit jar ring onto the bottom of your pet's bowl to prevent it from gliding on the floor while your pet is eating.

A puppy can be trained to stay away from wastebaskets. Just place a mousetrap in the bottom! Your pet will not be hurt when it goes off but will get an unforgettable scare.

Outdoor water bowls for dogs need never spill again. Drive a stake into the ground and slip a one-piece angel food cake pan down over it. Fill the pan with water. Your pet won't be able to spill it but the pan is easily removed for refills and cleaning.

You don't have to stand guard over your plastic trash bags to prevent the neighborhood dogs from tearing them apart before the trash collector comes. Put a small amount of chlorine bleach inside the trash bags before closing. The smell will repel snoopy pets.

BIRD-BRAINY IDEAS

Use a plastic mesh bag to hold ends of thread and yarn from sewing and other projects. Hang the bag outside during the spring and have fun watching the birds help themselves to the thread ends to build their nests.

To feed birds, cover a pine cone with peanut butter and roll in mixed birdseed. Tie a string around one end and hang.

Save old, unused barbecues for setting up as a bird feeder station. Keep bird seed in it during the winter.

Don't throw out last season's unplanted seeds. Place them in feeders for the birds.

Help the birds survive the winter by feeding them your excess meat drippings. Use a straight sided can as a container. Preshape heavy-duty wire (you can use a clothes hanger) to form a core for the drippings. Coil one end of the wire to fit the bottom of the can with the remainder forming a center stem. Now slide the wire into the can, fill the container with drippings and freeze. When ready, bend the top of the wire stem to form a hanger and cut the bottom lid off the can — but do not remove. Use the lid to push the suet and wire core out and hang on a branch. Enjoy watching the birds enjoy themselves.

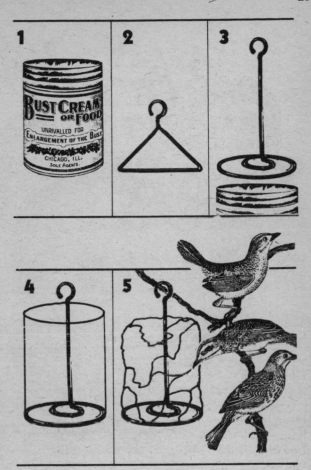

Chapter 2
KIDS ARE NOT BABY GOATS
more joy from parenting

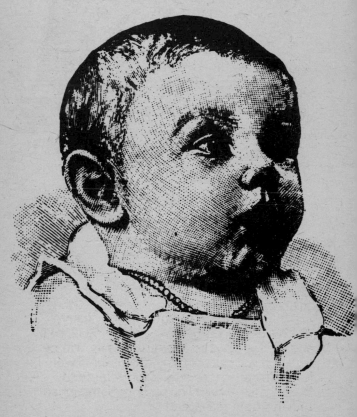

BATHING BEAUTIES

On chilly days before bathing your baby,
tumble dry the bath towel, receiving blanket
and clothes for a few minutes. They will be
nice and warm and fluffy. Both items will
have pleasant associations for your child.
Maybe they'll even continue to bathe when
they become teenagers!

While an infant is still too small for a baby tub, try a dishpan! Easier to handle and there's less room for your child to slosh around and possibly slip.

But for an even simpler method for bathing a baby, do the following. First, put a towel in the tub, then fill with water. Put a baby's carry-all in the tub and strap in the baby. Now the child can be bathed without holding the head up. Baby is more secure and happy. And you have both hands free to wash the whole child better.

To remove gum caught in a child's hair, soak the gum with rubbing alcohol. It does not harm the hair. The oiliness of peanut butter also does the trick (which tells you something about peanut butter.)

Bath time is the best time for giving your baby liquid vitamins. The dribbles will dribble right into the bath water.

Keep both shampoo and tears from children's eyes when bathing. Smear a little cold cream on their eyebrows and the soap and water wil take another route.

Prevent your children from scorching themselves when turning on the tub faucets while in the bath. Fill the tub first with hot water, then run cold water. If they do turn faucets on, the water will be cold, not hot.

My weight in Love I send

THE CHANGES IN LIFE

An inexpensive hat rack or shoe bag hung near a baby's changing table can hold washcloths, rubber pants, toys and other items for close reach.

Above an infant's dressing table erect a shelf for all those changing needs. Decorate the under part of the shelf with bright cut-outs that will entertain your child.

For diaper pins that are difficult to pass through diapers:

- Run the pin through your hair a couple of times. The natural oil is just enough to facilitate the passage of the pin through the diaper.

or

- Keep a bar of soap near the changing table and run the safety pins through the soap.

BEDTIME SOIREES

A beach towel is just the right size to make an easily washable mattress pad for a baby's crib. When the crib is no longer in use, recycle back to beach use.

If you're visiting a friend who has no crib available for your baby, you can put your child down on a big bed if—for safety's sake—you do the following. Put pillows on each side of the bed, but be sure you stuff them under the mattress. Your baby can't kick off the pillows or roll off the bed.

Instead of fighting a squirming baby to cut fingernails and toenails, do it while the baby is sleeping. It's faster and safer and easier.

If you've run out of clean pajamas for your child, use one of your old workshirts or T-shirts as a bed shirt.

Rx FOR A CHILD: TLC

When giving liquid medicine to an infant or
small child, it is very helpful to use an
eyedropper. Measure the prescribed amount
into the dropper and just squeeze into the
child's mouth. There is no spilling or waste of
expensive medicines and you are positive that
your child has gotten the exact amount
prescribed by your doctor.

When examining your small child's
sore throat, use a small lollipop as a tongue
depressor. As a reward give the child
the lollipop to suck on afterwards. It'll help
soothe the discomfort.

Medicine taste vile? Put an ice cube on your
child's tongue for just a moment before giving
the dose. The taste buds will be temporarily
de-sensitized and you won't need a spoonful of
sugar to make the medicine go down.

When youngsters need a splinter removed, have them hold an ice cube on the spot while you sterilize the needle. By the time you're ready, the finger will be momentarily but sufficiently numb for painless surgery.

Keep a supply of popsicles in the freezer for first aid. Youngsters who get a cut on the tongue or lip can use it to help stop bleeding, reduce swelling, ease pain. It tastes good and stops tears.

When children who are afraid of blood get a cut, wipe it with a clean red washcloth. They won't see the blood and if a stain does remain, it will not be detected.

Hand an egg timer to children whose temperatures must be taken. They can watch the passage of time and remove the thermometer themselves.

Give children with measles, chicken pox or with other itchy rashes a box of corn starch and a powder puff. They can powder themselves with corn starch instead of scratching.

FOOD AND THE SINGLE CHILD

Use an empty six-pack soda carton to keep baby's bottles and food jars organized in your refrigerator.

When feeding a child in a high chair, first place a large piece of old newspaper beneath chair. It protects the floor. Spills fall on the newspaper which can be discarded afterwards.

For children who will not eat gelatin because of the texture, let them sip it before refrigerating for jelling.

Puree leftover fresh vegetables in a blender. Freeze in ice cube trays and then wrap individually for the freezer. You'll have a perfect size serving for baby. The fresh vegetables have no preservatives or additives and they're economical, too.

When your young children are not feeling and eating well, try titillating their palates by serving them little bits of many things rather than a regular meal. Use a muffin tin and fill each segment with a small quantity of an appetizing food . . . a few french fries, a teaspoon of applesauce, several green beans. . . .

For snacking children, try the following combination: dip pieces of banana, peeled apple, orange or almost any fruit in honey and roll in wheat germ and/or ground nuts. It's nourishing and less expensive than "junk" foods.

A drinking glass is less likely to slip from a child's hands if several wide rubber bands are placed around the glass. Use various color bands to decorate and brighten the cup.

A simple technique to teach children sharing: when splitting an apple, a candy bar, a piece of pie, a sandwich, have one child cut and divide the item and the other child take the first pick. Rotate positions each time. No more cries of "bigger half," "me first," "no fair."

If there are two or more children and only one piece of pie left, instead of a squabble have a raffle and let the winner enjoy! (Drawing straws or picking a number from 1-10 works well.)

When serving mixed drinks to adults in the presence of children, include them in the festivities by giving them a soda with a slice of orange or cherry.

INDEPENDENT DEPENDENTS

Hang a small mirror low enough for your
young children in the bathroom. They will be
interested in keeping their face and teeth
clean if they can see what they are doing.

To get children into the habit of keeping their
faces clean at an early age, when they start
feeding themselves, give them a damp
washcloth along with the food. Then when
they spatter all over, they're more apt to
follow your suggestion to wipe their faces.

While teaching your children to dress
themselves, tape pictures of the clothing in
each drawer on the front of the drawers. In
that way they will know which drawer has
their underwear, which their shirts, etc. It's
also a good way to get them in the habit of
putting their clean clothes away in the right
space.

Empty shoe boxes in children's underwear drawers serve as compartments to keep like items organized, separate, and neat.

Prevent youngsters from removing the laces from their shoes; tie a knot at the end of each lace before you tie the bow.

Frayed tips of children's shoe laces can be renewed by clipping the ends. Then twist and dip in colorless nail polish.

Replace broken laces in children's shoes with crocheted laces to match the color of the shoes. They are stronger than regular laces so will last much longer.

If you want to avoid constantly replacing those rubbers and boots your child loses at school, dip a cotton swab in bleach and mark the boots with your last name (so boots can be passed on to siblings.) The bleach removes the color from the rubber. Of course, don't try this trick with white boots and rubbers.

For children's lined boots that get wet inside and need to be used before they dry normally, use the hose of an electric hair dryer as a blower. It takes only a few minutes before they are warm and dry.

Children will break fewer zippers if zipping is made easier for them. If you place a notebook ring through the hole of the zipper tab, it'll give the child a good strong loop to grab and pull.

CHILDREN-TO-GO!

Don't hesitate to take your infant who's still at the spitting up stage with you when you go out. Carry along a small baby food jar with a mixture of baking soda and water. Use it to clean spots and eliminate odor.

Embarrassed when your children get cranky in the supermarket? If you have a small box of dry cereal or some dried fruit in your purse or pocket, you may distract them and make them happy with your bring-along goodies.

Before starting out on that trip with the children, hang a shoebag over the seat of your car. Use the pockets to hold toys, crayons, tissues, slips of paper for coloring and writing and all those necessities and distractions that make a trip fly by for children.

When traveling by car with youngsters, always take a roll of paper towels for quick clean-ups and for instant diapers in case of emergency.

Taking a group of children to a show or any place of entertainment? Also take a large shopping bag in which you put all their hats, mittens, gloves and scarves. Saves lost time, tempers and tears.

PLAY: CHILDREN'S WORK

A baby's pacifier can be kept in close reach if a ribbon is tied on it and pinned to the child's pajamas or shirt.

Divert the attention of toddlers who have discovered "playthings" on the coffee table. Place their own toys on the corners of the table. They will play with them and leave your artifacts and conversation pieces untouched.

When very young children, who are learning to use crayons, want to color, they tend to draw on walls and other inappropriate places. To prevent this, when they have crayons, put them in a high chair. Later on insist that crayons with paper and coloring books be used only in a special place such as at the kitchen table—a time and a place for everything!

Use plastic net bags to hold your child's tub toys. Put the wet soapy toys in the bag; put under the faucet to rinse; and then hang on the faucet to dry.

Dry shampoo your child's stuffed animals with fuzzy coats. Rub in dry cornstarch and allow to set briefly. Then brush out. The toys will be clean and bright again and you'll prolong their lives by using this technique rather than putting them in the washing machine constantly.

When your children tire of their own toys, arrange a trade with friends or neighbors. After a few weeks you can switch back or proceed with additional rotation.

Before giving puzzles to small children, mark the back of each piece with a number or color. If pieces later get mixed up with other puzzles, the coding will make the sorting simpler.

If you're doing an outside painting job and your young children are anxious to participate, give them empty coffee cans filled with water, their own brushes and let them "paint" the bottom stairs.

Avoid roller-skating casualties. Adhesive tape on the roller-skate wheels will slow down the action and result in less adhesive tape and bandages on scrapes and cuts.

Are you teaching your children to be aware of time? If you place a clock in the window facing out toward the play area, the children won't have to constantly run in and out or call you to check the time.

KID CRAFT

Old greeting cards, postcards and pictures from magazines have numerous uses. Let us count some ways: 1) bookmarks, 2) decorations for gift wraps, 3) greeting cards, 4) collages, 5) mobiles, 6) decoupage, 7) picture books for children, 8) use your imagination.

In addition, make attractive hang tags for Christmas trees by pasting appropriate and pretty pictures and designs from old Christmas cards and magazines on both sides of plastic lids. Punch holes in the top of plastic lids, pull a 6-inch ribbon through each and tie.

Kids Are Not Baby Goats

Another kind of Christmas tree decoration
can be made with empty plastic containers.
Decorate lemon and lime concentrate
containers with scraps of yarn, felt, ribbons,
and sequins.

Other festive Christmas ideas: fill old baby
jars with candy. Make a Santa's cap for cover
and decorate the jars with a Santa face. Good
for X-mas party favors, stocking stuffers or
for a seasonal coffee table decorative candy
holder.

Save complete halves of walnut shells for Christmas tree decorations. Put a loop of gold or silver string through the top, glue back together and paint silver or gold.

Place coins inside the unbroken halves of walnut shells, glue together and paint. Use as stocking stuffers, in favor baskets for children's parties or as hand-outs for Chanukah "gelt (money)."

Instead of wiring pine cones together for crafts projects, glue them. Linoleum glue is the most permanent.

You can stimulate your child's interest in art and decorate his room at the same time with a constantly changing picture gallery. Just run a piece of strong cord across the bedroom wall and use paper clips to affix attractive pictures and interesting prints.

Chapter 3
DOMESTIC TRANQUILLITY
care of person and property

KEEPING THE DOCTOR AWAY

There are do-it-yourself permanents, and do-it-yourself manicures and also do-it-yourself teeth-cleaning! Once a month, dip a dampened cotton swab into baking soda. Use an up and down motion on each tooth with the swabs. Cheap, fast and effective.

When your gums bleed after a tooth extraction, use a wet tea bag as a compress. If the bleeding doesn't stop, call your dentist.

Prevent a red nose due to colds. Spread petroleum jelly on your nose before blowing.

A sore throat can be eased with the following potion: 1 tablespoon of black currant jam, juice of 1 lemon and a pint of boiling water. Stir well, cover and strain. After 1/2 hour stir in a little honey and enjoy.

Try this sure-fire remedy for laryngitis and/or sore throat: wet a hand towel in cold water; wring it out well; then wrap it around the throat securing it with a large safety pin so that the towel will stay tight against the throat. When the towel is no longer wet or cold, wet it again. The cold water reduces the fever and swelling. Simple!

Dilute the spiciness of red peppers and other spices by sprinkling salt in your mouth.

To relieve the pain and stop the swelling from a bee bite, apply a slice of onion.

Hiccup Help

Eat ½ tsp. of sugar.

or

Take one 1/2 tsp or more of lemon juice
(reconstituted or fresh). Gives fast results.

or

Take a glass of cold water, block your ears
while drinking it. To hold the glass while no
one is around, block your ears with your
thumbs and hold the glass with the rest of the
fingers on both hands.

To take away a bee sting—or insect itch—
moisten the afflicted skin and sprinkle with
meat tenderizer.

Vanilla extract applied to a burn will ease the
pain.

An instant ice pack for unexpected falls can
be found in your freezer. Take a package of
frozen vegetables—place in a plastic bag and
apply to injured area. (Quick, easy and ready
to use!)

A quick ice-pack can also be made by
filling a rubber glove with cracked ice. Tie
the wrist tightly and apply!

SAFE AND SECURE

On icy days when you don't want to wear boots, tape strips of adhesive tape to the bottom of your shoes to prevent slipping. (Technique is also good for toddlers learning to walk.)

Lightly sandpaper the soles of children's new shoes. It helps keep them from slipping.

When changing a worn out electric bulb, place the container from the new bulb over the old one and twist off. No more burned and dusty fingers. Bulb can be discarded right in the sleeve.

MEMENTO MORI

REMEMBER TO DIE

The lint from dryers is highly flammable and should not be recycled for stuffing toys or making pillows no matter how tempting or how strongly you believe in recycling!

In case of an accident or emergency, tape the blood type to the driver's license of each family member. List younger children's types, too, on each of the parents' licenses.

Flash grease fires in your oven? Don't throw water on it. Use baking soda which will smother the fire instead of spreading it.

Make your own kitchen fire extinguisher. Decorate a clean can with plastic tape. Fill with baking soda, punch a hole in the top and keep near the stove for sudden fires. The baking soda can later be removed.

Be sure you know what you're picking when berry-hunting in the woods. Many poisonous berries will cause you to itch.

Instead of using poisonous ant and roach killer in and around eating areas and children's rooms, use cinnamon. The smell repels insects and solves the problem.

In addition to putting a decal on windows where children sleep, as is frequently advised, the same should be done for rooms with elderly and handicapped people. These decals serve as an aid to fire-fighters in case of an emergency.

Ouch! Those nasty cacti prickles. If you've gotten them in your fingers, place a piece of masking tape over them for a few minutes, then peel off the tape. The prickles will adhere to the tape instead of your fingers.

Apply bathtub appliques on the bottom of all bathtubs to prevent slipping.

To make sure you get all the small splinters of shattered glass after breakage, go over the area with a piece of soft white bread. Be sure to wrap bread tightly after use and before discarding so children or animals don't get into it.

Other methods of gathering up small pieces of broken glass: pat them up with a dampened ball of absorbent cotton or a dampened bar of soap.

HEALTH YOURSELF

If you wrap a hot water bottle with aluminum foil it will keep hot longer.

For those who need to take lots of medication it is sometimes difficult to remember what has been taken at a given time. In the morning put the day's prescribed medication into separate cups. Put one cup inside the other in the order that they should be taken. At a glance you can tell just what's been taken and what not.

Those who use crutches should attach a canvas bag to one crutch to carry their belongings from one room to another.

To help a convalescent or bed-ridden person keep organized, set an ironing board to the right height and use as a tray over the bed. The board can be used for reading, hobbies, or anything they want to keep in easy reach.

Domestic Tranquillity

1 OZ. PREVENTION = 1 LB. CARE

To minimize possibility of forgery of your checks if stolen, have the name that is printed on your check vary slightly from your real signature. Example: use J. A. Smith on your check if your signature is Jane Ann Smith.

Make a photostatic copy of both sides of each of your credit cards and keep one set home in a safe place and carry another set when traveling. In case of loss or theft it eases the problems of identification and replacement.

To secure a purse on a car seat in case of quick stops or quick snatches, place a safety belt through the handle and fasten.

You'll always have proof of ownership of appliances and other valuable personal property in case of fire or theft if you take a picture of your TV and other treasures and place the pictures in a safe deposit box. The items will be easier to describe in order to locate and easier to identify when found.

ME, MYSELF AND I

Shake a small amount of talcum powder into the tub before taking a bath. It will smell good and prevent a ring from forming around the tub.

Keep the bathroom sink half full of water when cleaning dentures. If they happen to fall, the water will break the fall and prevent the teeth from breaking.

One cake of shaving soap can last over a year if you shave once a day. Compare its cost to that of a year's supply of aerosol shaving foams. 'Nuff said.

After shampooing oily hair, rinse with freshly squeezed and strained lemon juice. It will cut the excess oil and leave your hair squeaky clean.

The following procedure is not an alternative for medication. But to decrease dandruff combine 1/4 cup cider vinegar with 3/4 cup of lukewarm water and use as a hair rinse. Less flaky dandruff; nice shiny hair.

To give hair that clean, fluffy look without shampooing each day fill a squirt bottle with water, spot dampen hair, and blow dry. Especially helpful in eliminating a stubborn cowlick that may have developed during a night's sleep.

A quick way to clean combs and nylon bristle brushes: spray them with an instant cleaner and comb the brush gently before rinsing under hot water. And if you rinse them in a solution of water and fabric softener, they won't build up static electricity when they're used.

Whatever you call them—burdocks, stickers, prickles—when they get into your hair, they're a nuisance to remove. No, you don't have to cut big globs out of your hair. Just soften the burdocks with water and they'll come out easily.

After handling fish, seafood, or onions, put a liberal amount of salt on your hands and rub palms together for a minute or so. Wash with soap and water and the unpleasant odor will be down the drain!

Protect your hands when hanging out or taking in laundry from outdoors in cold weather. Wear a clean pair of white or colorfast gloves and you'll prevent chapped hands.

Nails brittle? Whenever you wear rubber gloves, place bits of cotton saturated in fingernail oil in each finger tip. While you're wearing the gloves, your nails will be oiled.

Common pitch from trees and cones can be removed from your hands with bacon grease. Rub on the sticky stains as if washing. Rinse and the pitch will be gone.

or

Put a teaspoon of peanut butter into the palms and rub in. Wash with soap and water. It not only removes the pitch, but softens the hands as well.

To remove tar from hands and clothing use baby oil on a cotton ball.

To get car grease off your hands, scrub with baking soda.

or

Combine 2/3 parts cornmeal to 1/3 powdered laundry detergent. Mix and work in well on wet hands. Rinse and the grease is gone.

Instead of using expensive face creams apply a little salad or cooking oil to complexion using cotton ball or finger tips. Leave on for a few seconds for the face to absorb and then wash gently with lukewarm water. Keep it on a little longer if your skin is dry. For an astringent rinse with water mixed with a few drops of cider vinegar to provide a natural acidity.

If you wear cotton gloves under rubber gloves your hands won't sweat or stick to the gloves.

Keep hands dry and smooth while doing dirty work by putting your hands into plastic bags. If interrupted, invert bag. Your hands stay clean. The bags can be discarded after use.

Bubble-bubble without toil and trouble! Make your own bubble bath. When your hand soap gets too small or breaks apart, place several pieces together in a metal rust-proof can in which you've punched holes on the bottom and lower half. Use string, wire, etc. to hold can on faucet. Run hot water at full pressure for a few seconds —there it is—bubbles galore. Most hand soaps have a perfume in them—so no need for those expensive bubble baths.

Make your own cleansing cream by adding corn meal to pure vegetable shortening until you get the desired consistency. No more allergic reactions to chemicals.

During hot humid weather keep lipstick in the refrigerator to prevent it from melting or becoming gooey.

Shampoo or a liquid dish soap are fine eyeglass cleaners. Do not use water. Wipe until clear. Added bonus: glasses will not fog.

Here's something a dollar will buy. If you have a dollar bill, you can clean your eyeglasses anytime.

When you've been out in the cold air and come into a warm house, prevent eyeglasses from steaming up by walking into the house backwards! (If you don't trip over something, you have it made.)

To prevent slips from crawling up while wearing synthetic garments, wear your slip inside out!

Scotch tape is a handy remedy for an undone hem away from home.

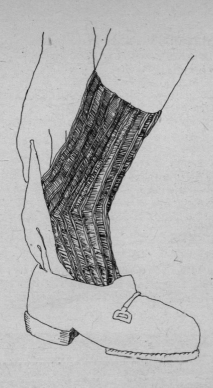

In lieu of a shoehorn, slip the end of a handkerchief in the back of the shoe. Hold the handkerchief taut. Pull! It acts as a track for your foot to slide right into the shoe.

When taking a bath or shower, start with a little cold water before putting on your hot water. You'll prevent your mirror or windows from steaming up.

Styrofoam trays that meats are packaged in can be cleaned and cut into the shape of the foot to make comfortable inner soles. Placed inside your boots, they retain your body heat and keep your feet warm. And you can't beat the price!

When leaving the beach remove sand from your body easily and smoothly with baby powder. It can be used on sandy feet before entering your car, too.

SOME GEMS

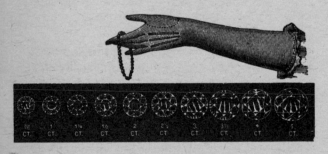

A piece of chalk kept in a jewelry box prevents the jewelry from tarnishing. An ounce of prevention saves a pound of jewelry polish.

To clean diamonds and other jewelry put toothpaste on a wet brush and scrub gently. Rinse and polish with a soft towel.

You can keep your pearls looking clean and lustrous by washing in warm soapy water, rinsing and drying. Do not rub with anything but a soft piece of flannel or a chamois.

If rings turn your fingers green, coat the inside of the band with colorless nailpolish.

To repair a broken necklace, re-thread it with lightweight fishing line.

It takes at least two to tangle! You can keep necklaces neat by taking old playing cards or other cardboard, make notches along the side, and wrap the chains around the card.

Keep thin chains from becoming tangled by slipping the chain through drinking straw and fastening the clasp. Use more than one straw for extra long chains. Cut straws to size for shorter chains.

If you have the right kind of wall space, make an attractive display from your costume jewelry chains. Take a piece of wood and hammer nails all over it. Paint or cover with paper color coordinated with your room or use a contrasting color for the nails. Now hang all those pieces of costume jewelry.

Adds an interesting note to the room decor and keeps jewelry organized. A sturdy piece of cork can be used in place of wood.

A clever way to clean difficult areas like jewelry boxes or dresser trays is to tie a piece of cheesecloth over the nozzle of a vacuum cleaner. It'll pick up the family dust but not the family heirlooms.

Chapter 4
FUEL-PROOF
energy-savers and energy-users

CRISIS CONDITIONS

Flashlights should be kept in a handy place for when the lights go out, but you can make them even easier to find if you put a strip of luminous tape around the handle.

When the lights do go out, you'll make fuse replacement a no-hassle job if you keep a supply of necessary size fuses next to the fuse box.

On cold nights be sure you pull your window shades down. The "dead air" between the window and the shade will serve as an insulator and you'll keep your room warmer.

If you unplug your instant-on TV to save electricity, when you plug it in again allow the set to warm up before turning on. If you don't, too much current will flow through your set all at once and destroy the tubes and circuits. Even if you don't unplug on a daily basis—do so when you're going away for weekends or vacations. The electrical savings will be worth it.

Retire five minutes earlier than usual each evening. Lights and TV off 5 minutes is a savings of energy. Multiply 5 minutes of energy savings days and think of how much money you save a year.

You can also conserve fuel if you turn the heat down an hour before bedtime. It takes about that long before the house becomes chilly. During a normal winter season the extra hour of lower temperature could amount to at least a full week's worth of fuel.

Rather than turn the heat up on extra cold nights, use sleeping bags. They're fun for a change, extremely warm, and think of how much easier it is to make the beds!

If you have electric heat with a separate thermostat in each room, keep the heat on only in those rooms most frequented. Also lower the temperatures in bathrooms and small kitchens since they retain enough heat from cooking and hot water usage as well as spillover from hallways.

Radiators and airconditioners work at optimum efficiency when filters and grilles are dust-free. Even thin dust layers block air-flow and act as insulation. Clean filters equal energy and money savings.

To reflect heat back into a room, place a sheet of aluminum foil behind each radiator.

Don't let the heat escape through your windows. Lined drapes provide insulation; plastic shower curtain liners also work.

You can also keep hot air inside your home on cold days by plugging cracks around windows, bottoms of doors, mail slots, exhaust fans, etc. with old towels and newspapers. For neater appearance use caulking compound.

Warm air won't escape up the chimney if you remember to close the flue when your fireplace is not in use. An open damper can result in a loss of as much as 20% of the warm air from one room in one hour.

FOOD FOR THOUGHT

Want to save cooking fuel? Use a pressure cooker. Cooking time for most foods is reduced to 1/3 the normal time. Examples of pressure cooker time vs. ordinary cooking time: fried chicken, 15 minutes vs. 45-60 minutes; pot roast, 35 minutes vs. 2-3 hours; pea soup, 15 minutes vs. 2-4 hours. Method retains important vitamins, too.

If you don't have a pressure cooker, apply some of the same principles for some of the same reasons: cook with very little water and tight lids. You'll save nutrients as well as cooking fuel.

Don't waste energy. Instead of parboiling beans, the previous evening put beans into a pot on the stove and bring to a boil. Turn off heat, leave covered, and let stand. They will soak all night in water and by morning will be ready for the additional ingredients and baking. You'll save 30-40 minutes of fuel energy time.

Cook frozen vegetables while roasting meat. Place undefrosted vegetables in heavy foil, add an ice cube for moisture and a pat or two of butter or margarine for seasoning. Close foil tightly. Vegetables will be ready in about 30 minutes. Leave unopened in the oven if dinner is delayed.

Elbow grease pays off in more ways than one. If you keep the bottoms of your pans spic and span, you'll save cooking fuel. Shiny, flat bottom pans attract heat faster.

Use your marbles! Save time lifting the top of a double boiler to check how much water is left. A few marbles placed in the bottom pot will make a racket when too much water is boiled off.

A LIGHT TOUCH

Use fluorescent rather than incandescent
lights wherever possible. Fluorescent lighting
uses less than a third of the electricity used by
incandescent bulbs for an equivalent length of
time.

Frosted bulbs inside frosted fixtures shed
much less light than you're paying for.
Replace them with clear bulbs for more
efficient service.

Because "long-life" bulbs give off less light
than standard units, use the former only where
light bulb replacement is difficult.

The high setting of a 3-way bulb is meant
specifically for reading. Use the lower settings
for general lighting purposes.

The thrifty time to change a light bulb is when it begins to look dark under the glass; otherwise, it wastes a good deal of electricity.

The price of decorator candles being what it is, it's questionable whether dining by candlelight is cheaper than electricity. However, candlelight dining *is* romantic and you can diminish the speed with which your candles burn by putting them in the freezer before using them. Frozen candles burn more slowly. Additional bonuses: less drip, less smoke.

CAR-FULLY

No matter what size your car, or how good the mileage, there's an economic, social and political need to conserve energy. Any driver can do so by maintaining a steady driving speed, accelerating gradually and driving within the speed limit for happy motoring.

To protect an exposed locked gas cap from ice and snow, stitch an elastic around the edge of a small plastic bowl cover and place over gas cap. On freezing days it's easy to remove and keeps the lock unfrozen.

Defrost a car door or car trunk lock by blowing heat on it with a hair dryer hose. (Of course you'll need to be within an extension cord's length of an electrical receptacle.)

Keep an old windshield wiper blade under the front seat of your car and use it when moisture condenses on the inside of the window.

A blackboard eraser is also useful for removing fog or steam from windows and windshield of cars. Keep one in your glove compartment.

But to eliminate the problem entirely, try this. A little glycerine rubbed on both the inside and outside of your windshield will keep the windows from fogging entirely during cold weather.

Wash your car with a dustmop head! Put your hand in the opening and wear it like a mitten. It makes a wonderful chamois-like wiper that can be washed and re-used.

And when you get to the white wall tires, try oven-cleaner. Works like a charm!

To remove rust and discoloration from the chrome and/or top of cars, crumple and wad a piece of aluminum foil (new or used), dip it in water and rub the affected area vigorously.

Remove scratches on cars with a crayon of the same color! It will also prevent rust from forming and spreading.

If you're really ambitious and want to remove some of those small dents and dimples, use a plunger. Place it on the dent and pull hard.

Never again swerve while driving because you were fishing for cigarettes, matches, or other small items. Just place a magnet inside the back of a pack or box and it will cling to the metal surface on the dashboard. An extra magnet placed under the ignition switch will hold reminders and turnpike toll tickets.

Sew a small magnet to each cuff of driving gloves. After each trip attach gloves by magnets to the dashboard of the car. They'll always be handy.

When you park your car in a huge parking lot, tie a bright ribbon or handkerchief to the aerial so you can spot your car in a jiffy.

If your motor continues to run after the ignition is turned off (called dieseling), turn the car off while in the drive position; shift to park and lock the key!

Even motor oil can be recycled! When you change the oil in your car, filter it through a cloth into a container. Use the old oil for the repair and maintenance of other motors, such as power tools.

During the winter season carry plastic gallon milk jugs filled with sand or ashes in the trunk of your car. They help weight it down and when you slide in snow and ice the gallon jug is an easy method for dispensing the sand or ashes. (If you have a choice, choose ashes. They tend to be more effective.)

Or instead of sand or ashes, carry an old piece of carpet in your car to put under the rear wheels if you get stuck in either snow or sand. It's neater than sand, takes less space and can be used repeatedly. After you've become unstuck, remember to retrieve your carpet.

OTHER MECHANICAL MONSTERS

Is your refrigerator or freezer operating at maximum efficiency? Make the following test. Close the door of your refrigerator on a slip of paper. If the paper pulls out easily, your door gasket is not tight enough and needs replacement to prevent the loss of cold air.

When rolling up a cord of a vacuum cleaner or similar appliance start coiling at the attached end. Never wind an electrical cord too tightly as the fine wires inside are vulnerable.

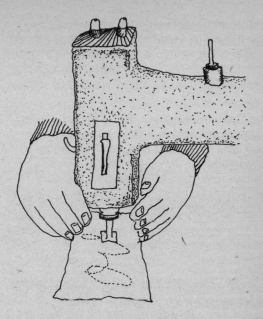

After oiling your sewing machine, sew through a blotter several times to soak up the excess oil.

If you don't have a humidifier, use an electric coffeemaker. Remove the basket and fill the coffee pot with water, plug in and watch it steam! The use of a humidifier in a room can help reduce the cost of heating, prevent dry throats and skin, preserve furniture and prevent static shocks.

When lawn mower and other small motors will not start, remove the spark plugs and put a few drops of gasoline into the hole. Replace the plug. Check to make sure it is in tightly. Repeat the procedure until the motor starts.

A tool for two seasons. Use a summertime lawn spreader in the winter to spread large areas with rock salt. Rinse well after use in both seasons.

A small label taped to an inconspicuous spot on your appliances can be used for a written record of repairs, date of last service call and the repairman's phone number.

The 3 S's: danger signals which apply to all appliances—shocks, smoke and smell—refrain from further use without check-up by a qualified person.

Give your air-conditioners a break. Place them in the windows on the shady side of the house. They'll play it cool-er, too!

Window air-conditioners need room for air circulation so keep shrubbery near the windows clipped and trimmed around the outdoor condensers.

Self-cleaning ovens, frostless refrigerators and microwave ovens do cost more and may even use more energy than simpler alternatives. But if time is your shortest commodity, they may be a bargain for you.

If you're an oven-peeper, you're an energy-loser. Each time the oven is opened you stand to lose as much as 25 degrees of heat.

Judge a flame by its color! If a gas flame in a hot water heater is yellow and not blue there is too much air in the combustion mixture and you're wasting energy. On a gas range a yellow flame means the burners may be clogged with tiny bits of food. Remove the burner and clean with a wire pipe cleaner.

When disassembling machines, such as sewing machines, for repair or cleaning, place all the removed pieces in a single tin plate or container. The effort will be worthwhile when you reassemble the machine and find all the pieces there.

Use your imagination and get double usage from your appliances. For example, pressure cookers can be pressed into service to complete a one-dish meal and coffee-makers with the insides removed can be used to cook asparagus standing up! Tie a string around the bundle. They'll stay together and be easy to remove.

A run-away power mower won't mow you down if, when tackling slopes, you cut them crosswise rather than up and down.

Save an old pair of tapered slacks for mowing the lawn—particularly if you use a power mower. They'll reduce the chance of loose fabric getting caught in the mower.

Believe it or not, a garbage disposal can get indigestion, too! It won't balk if you're careful about what you put down the drain and how much. Corn husks and pea pods tend to tangle so either skip the disposal for their disposal or mix them with other discarded peels and scrapings.

Here's an easy equation to remember while vacuuming. Once the bag is half filled then the more that goes into it, the less efficient the machine becomes.

Use an appliance to clean an appliance! Instead of risking an injury to the coils of a toaster or toaster oven, use the hose of a vacuum cleaner to remove any crumbs.

A steady hand makes for success. Your blender will give maximum power if you hold the container cover in place with your hand.

Chapter 5
A CLEAN SWEEP
the challenge of daily chores

KITCHEN CLEANING CAPERS

Fine grade steel wool found in hardware stores is of better quality and lasts longer than the pre-soaped kind. Just add a drop of liquid detergent. Steel wool costs considerably less than the pre-soaped kind and equals it in performance.

Household sponges can be washed in a clothes washer but do not put them in the dryer. They will harden, dry up and become stiff and useless.

Carry your household cleaners from room to room in an empty six-pack carton. Everything you need is on hand in one place and the handle makes it easy to carry from room to room.

Remove stains from plastic laminated counter tops in a kitchen by putting a bleach scouring cleanser on the wet stain. Let it stand and wipe to remove. So as not to scratch the surface, do not scrub.

Nail polish remover on a damp cloth will remove purple price mark stains from counter tops.

Melted plastic hardened onto a toaster or other appliances can be removed by gently using a razor blade to scrape it off the appliance when it is completely cold.

Finger prints and marks on stainless steel appliances can be removed if you apply a light coat of baby oil to the surface.

Make your own oven cleaner with the following recipe. Mix 1 cup white vinegar with enough baking soda to make a spreadable paste. Spread over the entire surface of the oven and leave on for 15-20 minutes. Wipe with a damp paper towel or cloth. Rinse with warm water and a clean cloth. It's safe and odorless.

Simplify the job of oven cleaning by removing one of the racks permanently. It's rarely used and can be inserted as needed.

To defrost an upright freezer, open the door and place a heater on a chair facing the freezer. The heat will accelerate the defrosting process.

Use the warm air from a vacuum cleaner hose to melt the freezer ice. Frost build-up puts a drag on the motor, so keep your freezer as frost-free as possible.

Clean under the refrigerator and stove without moving them by using a long snow removal brush, sprayed with a furniture polish. Pass the brush under the appliance; the brush will pick up all the dust.

Lemon oil cleans sinks, furniture, stoves and refrigerators. It's an economical way to get shiny clean appliances with less elbow grease.

Silicone car wax used on bathroom and kitchen appliances and fixtures will prevent water-spotting.

BATH MAT-TERS

To clean bathroom sinks, faucets, kitchen appliances and chrome, use a cotton ball or soft clean cloth which has been dampened with rubbing alcohol. When the alcohol evaporates, it leaves an instant shine.

If you keep a sponge under the soap in the bathroom or kitchen, it will catch the drip and allow the soap to dry. Use the soap-filled sponge for cleaning appliances and counters.

Avoid making the chore of cleaning the bathtub ring a bending and stretching exercise. Use a sponge mop sprinkled with detergent.

Stains from the tub or sink can be removed if you follow these instructions. Make a paste of cream of tartar, hydrogen peroxide and a few drops of ammonia and put on the stains in the tub or sink. Let set for 15-20 minutes. The stains will disappear.

A good way to clean grimy grout between tiles is to mix vinegar and dry detergent and make a paste. Apply to the tiles and grout with a cloth or old toothbrush. Rinse and relax!

or

Use a small brush with toothpaste or denture cream on the grout. Toothpastes usually have a mild abrasive which removes dirt. Works on porcelain, too.

An old toothbrush is the perfect device for cleaning a shower door track.

Mildew Memories

Remove mold and mildew in the shower by applying bleach with a sponge or brush on the tile surface. Let it dry a few hours, even overnight, then rinse with clean water. Dip a cloth in ammonia — either straight or diluted with water — and scour the tiles. Ammonia will kill mildew spores. Now wipe kerosene over the tiles. This allows the water to bead and helps prevent a build-up of scum.

Safety precaution: Never combine bleach and ammonia.

or

Step 1. Use furniture cleaner and scrub with a clean brush. After scrubbing, wipe away all the cleaner with cloth rags. This procedure removes body oils and soap film from the walls.
Step 2. Remove mildew fungus by mixing 1 gallon of tap water with one cup floor detergent and 1 cup chlorine bleach. (Use rubber gloves!) Scrub walls, using a small scrub brush in the corners and hard-to-reach areas. Let set for one hour. Scrub again with the same mixture and then wash off throughly with clear water. Let the walls dry completely.

Step 3. Apply a light coat of pure lemon oil furniture treatment with a soft cloth to seal the area. Let dry overnight. Special attention should be directed to grout joints and corners.

To keep mildew from forming in showers, hang a moth cake on the shower head. It is a good fungicide.

When cleaning tiles to destroy mildew don't forget to include the shower curtain. Let it soak in the tub in a water and chlorine bleach solution and then scrub.

Use baby oil to clean and shine fiberglass bathtubs and showers. Apply generously to a dry cloth and wipe. No need to scrub. The baby oil coating keeps the shine after many wipes. Have each member of the family get in the habit of wiping down the wall after each use.

WINDOW-WISE

To protect window sills from moisture, wax them — don't just wash them. They will only need dusting occasionally and rarely need washing.

When dusting venetian blinds slip an old pair of socks over your hands. They're less bulky than a dust cloth and allow you to dust behind the tape and under the slats. For metal blinds rubbing alcohol leaves a super shine.

To wash venetian blinds clean one slat at a time starting from the top and drying each one in turn. This prevents water from dripping and staining slats below.

When washing windows, use vertical strokes on the inside and horizontal strokes on the outside or vice-versa. "Goodby" to running in and out to clean the places you missed.

Instead of expensive window cleaners put rubbing alcohol into a spray bottle. It works just as well but is much cheaper. Vinegar and water or ammonia and water in a spray bottle are also effective.

This way to streak-free and film-proof windows: mix 2 tablespoons of corn starch in a small pan of lukewarm water. Stir frequently and use the mixture on a clean sponge to wash the windows. Wipe dry with paper towels.

The mixture of a few drops of kerosene in a pan of plain water is another window washing wonder. Windows will sparkle, dust and lint will not gather as quickly and the mixture is more economical than commercial spray window cleaners.

If Halloween pranksters mark your windows, remove the wax with lighter fluid and paper towels.

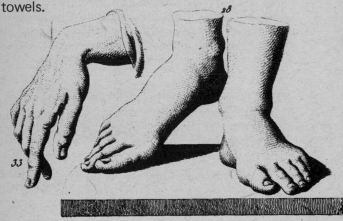

UNDER FOOT

Instead of shaking out a dry mop, lay it on the floor soiled side up. Step on the handle and vacuum the dust. Result: clean mop and happy neighbors!

A last-minute, hurry-up floor shine for tiles can be obtained by spraying on furniture wax and quickly buffing the tiles. It will be a temporary but on-time shine.

Black shoe marks can be removed from floors and linoleum: sprinkle a damp sponge with baking soda and wipe away the marks sans scratches.

Hair is nicer on pets than on possessions. To remove pet hair from rugs, stairway carpet and upholstery, use a large piece of contact paper, masking tape, clothing lint brush, damp sponge or sponge mop. They gather all the hair and can be discarded or rinsed out easily.

To remove grease from a carpet, brush dry baking soda or salt into a fresh stain and let it stand overnight The next morning vacuum the carpet. The stain should be gone.

When shampooing a rug, place plastic lids under the legs of the furniture. Remove after the rug has dried and you'll find that no deep impressions have been left.

Should indentations on rugs occur, hold steam iron over them for a few seconds.

Use small plastic cups that margarine comes in to move heavy furniture. Simply place the cups under each leg and any piece of furniture will slide easily across the carpet.

To prevent wooden chairs from scratching floors, place a small piece of self-stick carpet tile on the bottom of each chair.

An economical way to absorb oil or gasoline spills or drippings on the cellar floor, garage and driveways is to sprinkle kitty litter over the spot and let stand. When grease is thoroughly absorbed, sweep up.

Coffee grinds and kitty litter are excellent sweeping compounds for concrete floors. When dampened slightly, the compound picks up the loose dirt without raising the dust.

Eliminate the dirt from between slots of a radiator. Take a metal clothes hanger, slip a stocking over the end and clean.

or

Clean between radiator coils by using the same thin brush you use to remove snow from your car windshield.

FURNITURE FACE LIFTS

Save on furniture polish by covering a clean cloth with your favorite oil polish. Store it in a covered jar. Cloth can be re-used about three times.

Use brown shoe polish to cover any nicks or scratches on dark furniture. After a few minutes polish with a soft cloth.

Toothpaste on a wet cloth can be used to remove water rings on furniture.

Finally, a new use for corn pads besides keeping your feet in condition. You can keep your furniture unmarred by gluing corn pads onto the bottom of ornaments that might scratch the surface.

Delicate articles such as model boats and other items that are too fragile to disassemble can be cleaned by removing them from the shelves and spraying with a mild detergent. Let dry before replacing them.

SMELL AND TELL

Put a bar of lightly-scented soap into a vase
with your artificial flowers. Makes them smell
alive.

Remove stale or offensive odors from your
house while away by leaving out an open bottle
bottle of ammonia. By the time you return it
will be "Home, Sweet Home."

*Alternative Methods For Deodorizing Your
Home Quickly*

- Place 1/4 cup of real vanilla extract near the
  source of a bad odor. Absorbs the odor
  quickly.

- Boil small amount of vinegar on the stove.

- Simmer 1 cup of water with your favorite
  spice in a saucepan for 15 minutes. (For
  example, heat some whole cloves to rid the
  air of lingering skunk odors.)

- During vacuuming douse a cotton ball in
  cologne, aftershave lotion, or other
  deodorizer; place in the vent of the vacuum
  cleaner from which the air is expelled.

- Place disinfectant with water in a baby food
  jar in the vent of your floor to keep
  the small quarters of a mobile home or
  travel van smelling clean.

To Kill A Cabbage Odor

- Counteract the cooking odor of cabbage or cauliflower by placing one whole walnut, shell and all, in the pot with the boiling vegetable. If you are curious about where the odor went, open the walnut outdoors!

- A heel from a loaf of bread placed on top of of the odorous cooking vegetables absorbs the smell and can later be removed and discarded.

- To lessen the odor of cooking turnips, add a teaspoon of sugar to the water. The sugar will also make the turnips more flavorful.

Aluminum foil placed over a tray of ice cubes not only makes it easier to remove the cubes from the tray and prevent frost build-up in the freezer, but also keep the cubes from absorbing odors.

If fruit pies run over while baking, sprinkle salt over the spill. It will eliminate the burned odor and make it easier to scrape the charred sugar off the oven when cleaning.

Light a candle to clear the air of smoke and other offensive odors.

Leave a cut raw onion in a freshly-painted room room and the onion will absorb the paint odor. Cut off a thin slice from the onion from time to time to renew its effectiveness.

To deodorize paint add one or two tablespoons of vanilla extract to it.

A few pieces of chalk in drawers or storage boxes will absorb moisture and prevent mildew.

But if you do find your closets or drawers are mildewed, sponge with a solution of one cup baking soda to each pail of hot water. This solution also eliminates the smell of mothballs.

To rid clothes of the smell of skunk place them in a plastic bag with one pound of moth crystals or balls for 2-4 days. Then wash as usual.

Each time you empty your car ash tray put a layer of baking soda in the bottom to absorb the odor and help keep your car and clothes fresher smelling.

To keep chimneys free of soot, sprinkle salt-peter on the fire once a month. Also decreases chance of chimney fires.

Chapter 6
DISH-ORGANIZED
kitchen short-cuts

POTPOURRI

Experience is the best teacher. Whenever trying a new recipe, mark the date in the cookbook and any adjustments or substitutions made, such as more or less milk, higher temperature, an extra egg. After results have been tasted, make a notation as to how it came out. Keeps you from making the same mistake twice.

To hold a recipe card at better reading level, place it between the tines of a fork and place the fork, handle down, into a glass. It will remain clean, easy to read and out of the way.

Another method for keeping recipes handy while cooking: glue a cork on top of your recipe files. Make a slit in the cork and use it as a holder for the card you are using.

Keep bottle corks on hand to use as a pin cushion for loose tacks and pins that find their way into drawers.

Looking for a funnel to fill salt or pepper shakers? Use the corner of an envelope with a small portion of a corner tip cut off.

A corroded metal shaker top can be opened if soaked in a solution of hot vinegar and salt. The corrosive material will wash away after the top is removed.

For glass jars or bottle tops that are difficult to open:
> Hold them under hot water for a minute before turning. Pry up a corner of the lid to release the vacuum. Lid will turn easily.

An alphabetical arrangement of your spices on the shelf will facilitate location of a specific one as needed.

Transparent toothbrush tubes are ideal containers for metal or wooden skewers. Keeps them together neatly.

Handle slippery spaghetti smoothly! Make a "lip" by bending part of a colander. It'll be easier to transfer the spaghetti to a plate.

To prevent a cream pitcher from dripping, put a small dab of butter or margarine under the spout.

Poke the beaters of an electric mixer through wax paper before using. It prevents the mixture from splattering the rest of the beater unit.

For a convenient hand towel in the kitchen take a wire shower hook, stick the point through any small terry cloth towel or face cloth and hook it onto the handle of a drawer or on a closet hook.

For a family of four, paper napkins used at least three meals daily at 50¢ per package, per week, cost $25 per year. Instead, use gaily colored, small finger-tip towels. They can be used for several meals, washed repeatedly and you'll save and save and save!

When frying foods, cover the other stove burners with lids from pots and pans or aluminum pie dishes. The spattered grease will land on the washable covers and keep your stove top and burners clean.

Aluminum pie plates from frozen foods can be turned into burner liners. Cut to fit with heavy shears.

An oven mitt or potholder is handy for removing items from the freezer. When ice cubes must be twisted out of trays, the protection from freezer burn and comfort to your hands will enable you to give the tray the necessary twist.

Keep a clean powder puff in your flour box or canister. Handy for dusting flour on pastry boards, rolling pins, cake pans, etc.

When extra ice is needed for large gatherings, fill styrofoam egg cartons with water and use as additional disposable ice cube trays.

Find a home for your own home-made bread crumbs! Funnel them into an empty, spouted salt box. You might want to replace the salt wrapper with a washable scrap of wallpaper and label appropriately.

Use clean, squeeze-type catsup and mustard containers to decorate cakes. Their spouts are great for writing and drawing with icing.

Empty milk cartons are excellent containers for garbage. Open the top completely, rinse and store for use as needed. Generally leakproof, they can hold bones, grease and gravy. When filled, they will remain odor-free and waterproof.

Appliance cords can be stored attractively and neatly. Cover toilet tissue cardboard tube with pictures, wrapping paper or tape and use to store and label the cords.

Plastic wrap won't stick if it's kept in the refrigerator.

When you use your timer for baking, set it for a few minutes less than the specified time. Then you'll have a little extra time to stop what you're doing, get to the kitchen and to some potholders and remove your cake, cookies, pies, roasts from the oven. You can always let them bake an extra minute if necessary. Alas, if they're burned, it's too late!

CLEAN SCENE

Conserve both fuel and human energy while washing dishes. Stack as many items in the sink as possible and fill with steaming water. When the water cools, most of the dishes will have washed themselves without the use of running water. Rinse in cold water and air dry. But those that are apt to rust should be towel-dried immediately.

Soap pads tend to be larger than needed for most purposes. Once they're wet, they rust. Avoid waste by cutting them into smaller ones. Or simply break off a piece only as large as you need. You can discard after use;

the remainder is left for another time.

Oven still warm from cooking dinner? After washing dishes, place them in the oven for easy drying.

Before placing a greasy pot in the dishwater, wipe it with an absorbent paper towel. Now wet the pan, rub it with any bar soap 'til a lather forms. Wipe and rinse.

A teaspoon of dishwater detergent and hot water will clean a thermos bottle. Let it stand for a few minutes before emptying and rinsing.

You will need only one tablespoon of dishwasher detergent if you run the water faucet at the sink until the water is really hot before turning on the dishwasher.

Three capfuls of pine-scented ammonia added to the dishwater or dishwasher will give dishes a bonus shine.

Your dishwasher will work more smoothly and won't accumulate grease if you run it empty once every three months. At the rinse cycle, open, add one cup of liquid bleach and one cup of white vinegar and complete the cycle. If your glassware has become clouded, you can put it in the dishwasher at this point to make glasses sparkle once more.

The murky, cloudy look inside crystal decanters or bottles will disappear with this real, raw recipe:

Chop up a small raw potato or potato parings.

Put them in the decanter with a small amount of water and shake.

Rinse with clear water.

CRYSTAL CLEAR: Mix 2 tablespoons baking soda with one tablespoon dishwashing liquid and add to one gallon of water. Results: A shiny reflection!

Bottle too small to be cleaned with a bottle brush? Sprinkle a few pieces of uncooked rice and a pinch of salt in the bottle. Shake a few times and rinse. The rice and salt act as an abrasive cleaning agent and remove dirt from corners and sides.

Burned food

can be removed from pots

and pans any number of ways.

Try them all and identify which

is best for your own utensils.

Stainless steel

pots and pans

A combination of scouring power and kosher soap will not only clean but also shine stainless steel pots and pans.

All pots and pans

Fill with water and boil a few minutes. Add one or more tablespoons of baking soda to water and boil. Burned particles will lift out.

Aluminum pots

An aluminum pot that has turned black from boiling eggs can be cleaned by putting water and cream of tartar in the pan. Boil for five minutes and then wash.

Apples are not only for eating! Brighten dulled aluminums pans by boiling some apple parings in them.

Teflon-coated ware

Sprinkle baking soda and let stand for one Wipe clean. This method is scratchless.

Glass and ceramic ovenware

Put baking soda on stains

To remove coffee and tea stains as well as scratches:

Coffee and tea cups	Basin, tub and tile cleaner. It's non-abrasive so it will not harm dishes.
	One quarter cup of liquid bleach and 3/4 cup of hot water. Let stand for few minutes and wash. Save bleach by transferring from one cup or mug to another.
Ceramic/glass ovenware	Cream of tartar
	Vinegar
Aluminum coffee/tea pots	Fill pot with cold water and add 1 teaspoon baking soda. Bring to boil and allow to simmer 5-10 minutes. Clean with soap pad, wash and rinse.

Clean a blender by blending! Fill with hot water and dish detergent after use, rinse and see it sparkle!

After using a barbecue grill, use oven cleaner on it while it's still hot. By the time you're done eating, the grill will have had time to cool and it will wash easily.

To remove tarnish from silverware, soak it in bleach for one minute and then wash in hot soapy water.

Toothpaste will also remove tarnish. It's especially convenient if you're doing one small piece.

To remove any sticky substance from glass, formica, plastic, chrome or other metals try any of these remedies.

- Put fingernail polish remover on a cotton ball. Rub sticky spot. Keep away from eyes and mouth and be sure to wash afterwards.

- Rub with a pencil eraser. It will not mar the finish.

- Use lighter fluid on glass and metal only.

- Rubbing alcohol also dissolves stickiness.

One of the more efficient but less traditional ways of cleaning pewter is with a cabbage leaf!

Chapter 7
FOOD FARE
ways to prepare

FOR THE LUNCH BUNCH

To pack a simple hot lunch, fill a vacuum
bottle with hot soup and add one or two hot
dogs with a string tied around them. Let the
string hang out of the bottle for easy removal.
Pack rolls separately, then when the dogs are
added to the rolls, they'll truly be *hot* dogs!

If you put mustard between meats rather than
on the bread of sandwiches, the bread won't
get soggy.

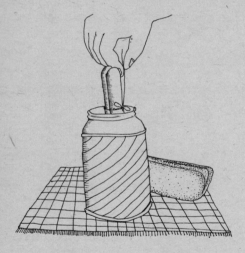

When putting a piece of frosted cake in a
lunch box, split the cake and make it into a
sandwich with the frosting in the middle; then
wrap. Frosting will stay sandwiched by cake
rather than rolled off by the wrap.

If the frosting must stay on the top of the cake, butter the wax paper slightly and the frosting will not stick.

For lunch pail cupcakes: bake them in a flat bottom ice cream cone. Fill with batter 3/4 full and bake a little longer than normal. For frosted lunch pail cupcakes: fill only half full, so that when frosted, the frosting is below the rim of the cone.

Packing cookies in a lunch box? Prevent their crumbling and breaking by placing pieces of cardboard between items before wrapping.

DOUGH DO'S AND DONT'S

When making cookies or doughnuts, you can use corn starch as an egg substitute: 1 tbsp. corn starch = 1 egg.

Save time and handling when making cookies. Roll dough right on the greased cookie sheet. Cut the shapes and remove the excess. Spades will remain spades.

Inexpensive and quick doughnuts can be made with frozen biscuit dough from pop-open cans. Poke a hole in the middle of each bisquit and stretch open. Deep fry in a small saucepan. Roll in sugar and glaze while hot.

When frying doughnuts, place one teaspoon of ginger in the oil. It will prevent the oil from saturating the dough; doughnuts will be light and fluffy.

One tablespoon vinegar added to a recipe for dough will insure its success.

As soon as you remove bread and cookie dough from the bowl in which it was mixed and the board on which it was rolled, sprinkle salt on the used utensils. Remnants of the sticky dough will wipe away easily and quickly.

If you've run out of flour and the dough you're rolling is sticking to the board, sprinkle the board and rolling pin with sugar. It not only does the trick, but adds a hint of sweetness to the dough.

If you have the filling, but not the dough for a pie, use white bread slices. Believe it or not, it's delicious! Good for one-crust pies.

Powdered cream substitutes can be brushed on a pie crust in lieu of milk for a nice brown effect.

If you're baking three pies or breads, but your oven isn't large enough to accommodate them all at once, place a brick on its side between the two pies on the bottom of the oven. The brick will be higher than the pies, and the third pie can be baked on the top of the brick.

Get clean, unragged slices from a meringue by sprinkling granulated sugar over the meringue.

To prevent pie crusts from over-cooking and
the juices from burning, place strips of wet
cotton or aluminum foil, one inch wide,
around the edge. If you use foil, tuck it under
the edge of the pie plate.

When baking a berry pie, insert a piece of
macaroni or a metal tip from a cake
decorating set into the center. It will act as a
chimney, allowing the steam to escape, and
preventing the juice from bubbling over onto
the oven.

Sprinkle a little baking soda over the fruit in a
pie before putting on a top crust. The juice
will not runneth over!

Either a pinch of baking soda or a pinch of
salt, added to rhubarb or apples when making
sauces or pies, will neutralize the acids and
decrease the amount of sugar needed for their
preparation.

Keep peeled apples from turning brown by soaking them for 10 minutes in moderately salted water or water with 2 tablespoons vinegar.

Bake fruit bread in #1 coffee cans. Grease well, fill half full and bake. The bread can be stored right in the can. Use the plastic lid as a cover to make the container airtight.

Use greased aluminum foil instead of waxed paper or a moist towel when letting bread dough rise. The foil holds the heat in and quickens the rising time without souring the bread.

When making bread, put dough in pans and place them on a heating pad with the switch turned on "low" (about 80 degrees). It will provide a warm spot for the dough to rise and double in bulk.

If your home is at a temperature too cool to allow bread to rise properly, place the dough in the oven and turn on the oven light. The 40 watt bulb will bring the temperature up to 80 degrees. The isolated environment will also prevent drafts so the yeast will do its thing!

To prevent crust from getting brown and hard when baking bread, place a pan of water in the bottom of the oven.

Soften the top of rolls after baking by brushing lightly with one tablespoon of sugar dissolved in three tablespoons of cream after removal from the oven.

Rolls and muffins which have hardened are easily freshened by sprinkling them with water and placing them in a hot oven for a few minutes.

Your muffins will never scorch if — when filling the tin with batter, you half fill one empty muffin cup with water.

Use an ice cream scoop or a half-filled soup ladle for transferring batter to cupcake tins.

Make your own cake flour by putting a teaspoon of corn starch in a measuring cup and filling the cup with unsifted all-purpose flour. One cup of this mixture is the equivalent of one cup of sifted cake flour.

HOW SWEET IT IS!

When a recipe calls for molasses, maple syrup
or other sticky ingredients, measure the
shortening first. Use the same measuring cup
for the sticky substance and it will pour out
with no mess.

Save the additional cost of confectioners
sugar; make your own! Pour granulated sugar
slowly in the blender as it operates at the
highest speed. The longer you blend, the finer
the sugar.

When whipping cream, use confectionery
instead of granulated sugar. Since it prevents
the cream from separating, you can make
whipped cream ahead of time, refrigerate it
and relax at your next party.

To remove citrus peels easily, heat fruit in the oven for five or ten minutes. Skins will slide off the fruit.

The warmer the lemon, the easier to extract the juice. So heat lemons in hot water before squeezing to get just as much juice as possible.

Crush fruits for jams, jellies, preserves and desserts in a blender.

Want to keep nuts and fruits from sinking to the bottom of your baked cake? Heat the fruit and nuts, roll in flour, add to batter and they'll stay evenly distributed.

Cut dates, prunes or raisins without getting sticky fingers by first rolling the fruit in flour and then cutting them with kitchen scissors or knife.

Scrape a small apple into the batter of a cake to keep the cake moist longer and improve its flavor.

If you need a smaller cake pan than you have, fold heavy duty aluminum foil to proper size, place in larger pan, using at least two sides of the pan as supports. Fill foiled area and bake.

Use white sugar to flour a cake pan and your cake will never stick.

Rather than dusting cake pans with flour, use cocoa for chocolate cakes, and bread crumbs for lemon, orange or strawberry cakes. They'll give the cake a beautiful brown color and prevent sticking.

To keep cakes from sticking to the bottom of the pan without using oil and flour, simply wet brown paper bagging, cut to fit and line pan bottom.

For flatter layer cakes, pour the batter in a ring around the edge of the pan and smooth a little toward the middle. Many people have problems with the flatness of their cakes because they tend to pour directly into the middle of the pan and spread it out from there.

If the consistency of frosting is too thick for spreading, it will roll back. Place the frosting in a warm oven for a few minutes. The frosting will soften and spread easily without picking up crumbs from the cake.

To hold birthday candles on a cake, use miniature marshmallows. They protect the frosting from dripping wax. For winter motifs, they resemble snowballs.

You, too, can make a festive cake for a child's birthday! Make animal shapes in the side of a cake with cookie cutters. Frost shapes in contrasting colors to suggest a merry-go-round.

Also for children's birthday parties, decorate ice cream cones with a cherry or candy and then freeze. When it's time to serve the youngsters, everyone can be served immediately.

Even when you're having adult company the same basic trick works — expecially if you're anxious to dish out equal portions. A nice bonus is that the hostess can enjoy dessert at the same time, too!

When making fudge, use an aluminum ice cube tray into which to pour the batter. After it is completed, press the divider into the candy to make the squares.

To remove whole nutmeats from the shell, pour boiling water over the nuts and let stand overnight before cracking.

Keep peanut butter on an open-faced sandwich from sticking to the roof of your mouth! Turn the bread upside down and eat!

For popcorn balls on a stick, use a small lollipop on which to form each ball. It will be easier to eat and there will be a nice surprise waiting inside.

VARIATIONS ON A VEGETABLE THEME

Potatoes bake faster if each is set on end in a muffin tin. Remove the tin and you have all the potatoes at once.

After boiling potatoes, drain the water but leave them in the pot for a few minutes. The heat will harden the outside and prevent soggy potatoes.

Baking potatoes? Soak them in cooking oil and salt very generously. Bake at high heat. The skin will become the yummiest part of the potato.

1/2 teaspoon of baking powder added to mashed potatoes will keep them white. (Works also if added to grated potatoes for potato pancakes or potato pudding.)

When making scalloped potatoes, use half milk and half light cream. The sauce will boil, but not curdle.

If french fries are dipped in a mixture of lemon juice and water before frying, they won't become soggy.

Rather than scraping and nicking your fingers peeling winter squashes, first place them in a pan of boiling water for a few minutes, then put them in cold water and they'll be as easy to peel as a potato.

The bitterness of cucumbers can be just a memory. Cut off the ends and rub cut piece against the open end in a circular motion. A white foam will form. Rinse it off and the bitterness will be washed away. Do the same to both ends.

After buying a head of lettuce — wash, core and break into pieces with your hands. A knife will cause it to turn brown. Store lettuce in an airtight container with a piece of paper towel. The towel absorbs the moisture and actually makes the lettuce more crisp than when it was bought.

Chopped onions without tears! A piece of bread crust held between your teeth will absorb the acrid fumes. Refrigerating onions before chopping also does the trick.

Apples and peppers baked in a well-greased muffin tin will hold their shape!

If vegetables such as turnip and squash get soggy while cooking, add some instant potatoes for thickening. It won't affect the flavor.

When boiling macaroni or spaghetti, add a tablespoon of oil to the water to prevent sticking.

To rid rice of starch, put in a sieve and place under running water. It's easier than washing in a bowl.

Water, in which rice has cooked, makes an easy self-thickening gravy.

Get rid of the excess fat from gravy quickly by placing a few ice cubes into the liquid. Fat will form around the cubes which should be removed immediately.

Give your gravy an instant tan! Add color to pale meat gravy with 1/2 teaspoon of instant coffee to about one cup of gravy.

PROTEIN POINTERS

Pan-broil your steak or hamburg by using a layer of salt in the pan instead of grease!

Instead of using fat or oil to brown meat, use 1 or 2 tablespoons of liquid, such as water, broth or soy sauce. As the moisture evaporates, it draws the fat out of the meat. Yours for cheaper and healthier eating!

A piece of bread placed in the drop pan before broiling will absorb the grease, avoid flash fires and make for easy clean-ups.

Instead of frying meatballs for spaghetti, place them on a cookie sheet and bake in the oven. They needn't be watched constantly allowing time to prepare other elements of the meal.

To tenderize beef, brush all sides with a small amount of vinegar. Let it set for five minutes before cooking.

The fastest and easiest way to separate bacon just taken out of the refrigerator is with a rubber spatula.

Before frying bacon sprinkle corn starch into the frying pan. No spattering grease and crispier bacon!

When preparing a leg of lamb for roasting, insert a piece of macaroni in the slits where you have put cloves of garlic. After the lamb is cooked, the macaroni markers will be your guide for finding and removing the garlic.

When roasting poultry, place the poultry on a rack in the roasting pan with 1-1/2" water. As the poultry cooks, the fat will drop into the water rather than spattering. The water will keep the bird moist and succulent. The drippings can be used as a gravy base.

No more need to close a stuffed bird with stitches or trussing nails. Take the crust or "heel" from a loaf of bread and block the opening.

Make your own coating for fish or chicken by blending crackers and seasonings. Experiment with different herbs and spices for exotic flavors while using up stale crackers and bread for the crumbs.

To make fried foods such as chicken or shrimp more flavorful, try coating them with pancake mix instead of flour for a change of taste.

If boiling lobsters live seems cruel to you, put them to sleep for a few minutes in a sinkful of warm water. Then place in boiling water to cook.

To open clams, drop a few at a time into boiling water. Remove after 15 seconds. The hot water relaxes the muscle and permits you to slip a knife in between the shells.

EGGSTRA! EGGSTRA!

Want to keep track of which eggs in your refrigerator are fresher? Buy a dozen brown one week, a dozen white the next. You can tell instantly which are which.

Check the freshness of eggs by submerging completely in water. If fresh, an egg will lie on its side at the bottom of the container. If it rises slightly, it is still good for cooking, but if it stands up, it should be returned to the store for a refund.

Try another freshness test for eggs you crack open. Inside a really fresh egg, the shell will show a small air bubble about the size of a dime. The larger the air bubble, the older the eggs.

A foolproof way to separate yolks from whites is to crack the egg into a small funnel. The white will run through, while the yolk stays behind.

In decreasing a recipe, how do you cut the egg in half? Here's a rule of thumb. Beat the egg slightly. 1-1/2 tablespoons equals 1/2 egg; 1 tablespoon equals 1/3 egg. Save the rest for tomorrow morning's omelette.

When beating egg yolks and whites separately, beat whites first and shake the beaters well. No need to wash and dry beaters before beating yolks.

You can prevent eggs from cracking during boiling by allowing them to stand a few minutes in very warm water before putting them in boiling water.

But if an egg does crack during boiling, add a little vinegar to the water to reseal it.

When you are hard-boiling eggs to be used later, put a few drops of food coloring in the water. This will tint the shells and you can tell the cooked eggs from the uncooked immediately.

To prevent the greenish ring from forming on hard-boiled eggs, remove the fully-cooked eggs from boiling water and immerse in cold water immediately.

If your cold, hard-boiled eggs are difficult to peel, place them in a pan of hot water for 15-20 seconds; then peel.

When cutting hard-boiled eggs, dip your knife into hot water for beautiful, clean slices.

A dough blender is a handy tool for chopping eggs.

SPICY TIDBITS

A thoroughly cleaned spray bottle makes a great dispenser for oil. Use it to spray just the right amount of oil in salads, to grease pans and to add limited amounts to food while cooking.

If your griddle gets too hot when frying pancakes, rub a raw potato over the griddle to prevent the pancakes from sticking.

When cooking with spices such as garlic, bay leaves or peppercorns, which must be removed, place them in a tea ball. It's easier than a cheesecloth.

Ketchup can be used to the last drop — if you can get it out! Add enough lemon juice to dilute, horse radish to taste, shake well and you have a tasty seafood sauce.

When making ice cubes for iced tea, add lemon juice — and a piece of peel for attractiveness — to the water. There you are, tea with lemon!

Flavor drinks such as iced tea, coffee and cocoa by quickly making a syrup of equal parts sugar and water. Cook until the sugar has dissolved. DO NOT BOIL. Place syrup in jars or dispensers and keep in the refrigerator, ready for use at a moment's notice.

Fill emptied but unwashed jam and jelly jars with milk. Cover and place in the refrigerator. When the jar is clear of jelly, the milk is beautifully sweet. Use it as a drink or pour it over some cereal.

Prevent coffee grounds from entering your percolator by putting a thin piece of paper toweling in the bottom of the basket.

Oversalted food can be adjusted if you make an additional amount without salt and mix together. Divide; use one portion and freeze the remainder for future use.

If soups or other liquids are too salty, add a piece of raw potato and boil for five or six minutes. The potato will extract some of the salt. If still salty, repeat with another or larger piece of potato.

Chapter 8
CONSERVE AND PRESERVE
extending the versatility of food

FRESH

FREEZING COLD

For freshness, keep the following items in the freezer: a) potato chips, b) crackers, c) nutmeats, d) shredded coconut.

Package all foods for freezing in wrap (paper or plastic), bags, boxes or containers specifically made for freezing. Such wraps are moisture-vapor proof and will maintain product quality.

Before freezing food in freezer bags, suck out the excess air with a straw. You'll preserve the frozen food better.

Plastic margarine bowls and other plastic tubs are excellent freezing containers for short time storage.

Use the divided aluminum pans from TV dinners for making your own homemade frozen dinners. Fill compartments with leftover entrees and side dishes. Wrap in freezer wrap or slide into freezer bag. Label and freeze. Heat and use some night for a pot luck dinner.

You can freeze whole fish and prevent freezer burn by placing the clean fish in an empty milk carton. Fill with water to within two inches from the top. Staple or tape, label and date. This method allows fish to be kept frozen up to a year or more.

Well washed plastic lids from a coffee can or other containers should be put between hamburger patties before freezing. When needed, the patties will separate easily.

Left-over pancake batter? Make into extra pancakes immediately and freeze. Wrap separately for easy separation. Heat and eat a quick Sunday breakfast any day of the week.

Once you open a can of maple syrup, pour it into a small plastic container and place the unused portion in the freezer. It won't turn moldy and the syrup will return to its original thickness at room temperature. You can keep syrup for several years in this way.

To freeze whipped cream, drop by tablespoonful on a cookie sheet, and then put in the freezer. When frozen, place in a container or freezer bag for future use.

Freeze fresh parsley, greep peppers and green onions. Just wash each and put into plastic freezer containers. If the onions and peppers are pre-chopped, they'll be ready for use whenever you need them for cooking.

Waste not and have it when you want it. Bananas that are too soft for eating can be frozen in freezer bags or containers for future use in baking.

It comes as a surprise to many that lemons can be frozen. Slice and spread on wax paper and put in the freezer for 1/2 hour. Gather slices, place in a plastic freezer bag, and store

in freezer. Sliced lemon will always be on
hand for iced or hot tea or for a recipe.

Grate rind from lemons and oranges before
squeezing for juice and place in containers
in freezer. You will always have citrus
rind when needed for recipes.

Instead of going through the process of
canning tomatoes, just freeze them. Drop in
boiling water to remove skin easily, then put
them in ice water until cold and freeze in
freezer bags or boxes.

Eat "fresh" corn on the cob all year long by freezing them when they are the cheapest and sweetest. Put only one or two ears in each freezer bag to maintain quality.

To defrost food slowly, place in a styrofoam cooler or between styrofoam trays.

YOU CAN, TOO!

When canning or making jams or jellies which require hot jars, put them in a warm oven and they will remain warm until ready for use.

Make it easy to remove paraffin from homemade jellies. During the canning process, place two ends of a piece of twine, tied into a loop large enough to fit over the finger, in the liquid paraffin. When hardened, the twine will be a good pull for removing the whole unbroken piece of wax.

FRESH AS A DAISY!

You can preserve meat without freezing. Place meat in a bowl with a tablespoon of garlic salt, three tablespoons of paprika, one half teaspoon crushed red pepper and one cup of red table wine per pound of meat. Cover. Refrigerate. This method will not only keep your meat fresh for up to a week but will also tenderize it.

Keep leftover tomato paste usable and egg yolks soft and fresh by pouring a little salad oil over them before refrigerating.

To retard mold from appearing on a partially used container of cottage cheese, flatten the cottage cheese so it is smooth and level on top. The same process will prevent the liquid in sour cream and yogurt from separating.

If refrigerator crisper drawers are lined with foil or paper toweling, they will keep the fruits and vegetables even crisper.

No more soggy salads even though you've prepared them in advance. Place a saucer upside down in the bottom of your salad bowl and the salad will remain crisp.

To retain the freshness and crispness of peeled potatoes and cleaned carrots, place them in a glass bowl of cold water and keep refrigerated until needed for cooking. Process prevents vegetables from turning brown. Cook in same water to preserve water soluble vitamins.

In spite of what the banana growers say, if your bananas are getting ripe, place in the refrigerator. They will turn brown on the outside, but the inside will maintain its natural color and cold bananas slice easily.

To keep lemons fresh for months and ultimately yield more juice, place whole lemons into sterilized jars. Cover with cold water, adjust rubber rings and screw on cover tightly. Refrigerate.

Place parsley in an attractive glass or bowl with water and use as a kitchen table center piece. The water rejuvenates the parsley and keeps it fresh and crisp.

To store carrots for winter, cut tops to 1/2" above carrot top to prevent further growth. Put about 2" of sand in a box or other container. Alternate layers of carrots and sand ending up with sand on the top. Store in a cool spot. Carrots will be as fresh and crisp during the winter as when they were first picked.

Keep your potatoes from sprouting by placing an apple in with the potatoes.

There's a simple way to keep bread, potato chips, cookies and crackers in plastic bags airtight. Make slits in plastic lids from margarine or other bowls and slide the ends of the plastic wrapper through.

or

Twist excess wrapping tightly. Bring the wrapping above the twist—down around the bread. The smaller the loaf, the more wrapping there is around the bread.

or

Use a clip clothespin or twist to keep the package securely closed.

After unwrapping quarter of butter or margarine, place wrappers in the refrigerator and have handy for greasing pans or cookie sheets.

Prevent spilling and waste by taping the holes of salt, pepper and spice shakers when refilling.

Cookies and brownies can be kept moist by putting them along with several slices or ends of bread in a jar or canister. The moisture from the bread will keep them chewy.

To "reclaim" brownies or cupcakes that have been overcooked or become dry and hard, set the oven at 200 degrees, place the pan of goodies in another pan of water and cover with a few damp paper towels. Or put the cupcakes into a damp paper bag, close and place in a moderate oven. When the bag is dry, remove from the oven.

Recipe for softening marshmallows or keeping them soft: place a piece of bread in with the marshmallows, the moisture from the bread will soften them.

BROWN SUGAR BONANAZA

BROWN SUGAR

5 lbs.

FULL WEIGHT GUARANTEED

Ways to Keep Brown Sugar Soft

After opening the package, rewrap the remainder tightly and store in a bread box.

Put a few prunes in the container. It also sweetens the prunes.

Place a piece of lettuce in the package.

Keep in the freezer and allow ten minutes to defrost.

Put it in a plastic bag and sprinkle some water over it. Tie the bag tightly. In a couple of days, check to see if more water is required. Squeeze once in a while to break up the block of sugar. After it is all softened, refrigerate in an airtight container.

Place it in the top of a double boiler and heat until soft and then keep in airtight container.

Common denominator for all these methods: provide a moist but airtight container.

CRUMBY IDEAS

Keep the crumbs from the bottom of cookie boxes, bags, or a cookie jar in a covered container and use them in recipes calling for cookie crumbs. They also make a delicious topping for ice cream.

If homemade bread comes out undercooked, cut the bread into crouton size pieces and rebake at 200 degrees until crunchy. Use for salads or soup. Overcooked bread can be cut and blended or ground for bread crumbs.

Leftover pie crust or frozen bread dough can be turned into tasty rolls. Roll out the dough, butter it, and shake brown sugar & cinnamon on it. Roll up into a long roll and bake at 400 degrees till brown. They're great with coffee or milk.

Give stuffed leftover eggs a new flavor. Add sweet relish to them!

A STOCKPOT OF STANDBYS

Save the liquid from a jar of sweet pickles and add carrot sticks. Store in the refrigerator for two or three days. Use for snacks or serve as pickles. To any kind of pickle juice add slices of onion and use the same way.

Leftover pickle juice, used as part of the liquid for dissolving gelatin, adds a distinctive taste to molded vegetable salads. The spicy juice makes the tangy difference.

To re-use extra baked potatoes, first dip them in hot water and then reheat in a moderate oven.

Want a quick, nourishing, good tasting and economical lunch? Place leftover vegetables in the blender. Add a can of consomme or other soup of your choice. (Tomato is especially good!) Whirl a few seconds, add water or milk, heat and serve.

Save all the peelings and bits of apple from pie making. Boil, strain and make a small jar of jelly.

After a turkey meal, don't wrack your brains for new ways to titillate your family's palate. Slice the remains. Package the stuffing, white and dark meat separately and freeze for later use in sandwiches, salads and casseroles. Boil the carcass for soup and freeze the liquid until you are ready to make a turkey base soup. Nothing need be wasted by a family temporarily tired of turkey.

Buy large economy size cans of fruits, vegetables, soups, tomato sauce, etc. After opening put unused portion in small plastic freezer containers and freeze. Remove and use as needed or split with a friend or neighbor and avoid storage problem. Net result: great savings in money by buying in quantity.

Reheat all meat, potato and vegetable leftovers together in one large pan. Place foil between items. You've just saved two extra pans to wash!

Instead of discarding leftover gravy, keep a large container in the freezer and add whatever is left each time. This frozen stockpot gives you infinite variations when making a pot of soup or stew.

Place extra spaghetti sauce in ice cube trays and freeze. Remove as much or as little as needed for future recipes. Particularly good for individual child-size portions.

Pour leftover coffee into an icecube tray and freeze. Use a cube in a glass of fat-free milk for flavor. Refreshing drink for hot days!

or

Use the frozen, coffee-flavored ice cubes to make coffee gelatin. Served with whipped cream, it makes a delicious but not-too-sweet dessert.

Chapter 9
A SECOND LOOK
home renewal and recycling

A BRAND NEW COAT

Geographic locations should determine the color you paint your house. Light colors reflect the sun and keep the house cool. For colder climates darker colors happily absorb the sun's heat.

When papering or painting a room, use the light switch as a memory bank. Write on the back of the plate the date the room was done, the amount of paint used and/or the number of rolls of paper. No more guess work . . . all the information is there. In any case, keep that information for each room in a specific place you'll remember when you need it.

Save old plastic tablecloths to use as drop cloths when painting. For a large area sew or tape one or more together.

Once a can of oil-base household paint has been opened, a crust usually forms on the top. Secure the top tightly, turn the can upside down, and allow the crust to form on the bottom of the can instead of the top. No more mess of chopping through the crust to mix the paint.

Paint won't drip down the outside of the can if you use a large nail or screwdriver to punch three or four holes in the groove on the top of the can. It will drip back into the can instead.

Before pouring paint into a roller pan, line the pan with tin foil. When your job is done, discard the foil and the pan is clean for the next paint job.

When painting a wall near wall-to-wall carpeting, use an old venetian blind slat as a guard against the paint. Wedge the slat between the carpet and the baseboard. Wipe the slat each time and move on.

If you're painting doors, put some petroleum jelly on the hinges and you'll be able to remove the paint spatters from them easily.

That old fashioned protective remedy against insect bites, oil of citronella, will also keep the "critters" away from your freshly painted surfaces. So when you're painting outdoors, add a tablespoon of the citronella to a gallon of paint. Mix well before using.

Wash your paint roller cover with fabric softener and it will dry soft and fluffy.

During a large painting project you don't have to rinse, soak or completely wash the brushes each day. Just clean the brushes of excess paint, wrap in aluminum foil and place in the freezer until you resume painting. They'll be ready for work at the same time you are.

Paint brushes will retain their bristles and their shape after use if they are cleaned, squeezed dry and then wrapped in heavy paper towels.

To keep brushes especially pliant after use, clean, dry and cover with petroleum jelly. When needed for use, just wash.

Before storing, mark the level of what remains with a stripe of the same paint on the outside of the can. Now you won't have to open a can to determine what and how much paint is left.

Make your own funnel by cutting a plastic bleach jug in half. The top can be used as a funnel with a handle. The bottom can be used as a pail to clean paint brushes or store items. The funnel is handy for pouring paints into other containers.

Paint can be removed from glass with hot vinegar.

Shower caps make great painting hats. Just make sure all your hair is tucked in before you start painting.

And you might try wearing rubber gloves with turned up cuffs when you're painting. The drips will dribble down into the cuffs and protect your hands and the rest of you from getting covered with paint.

Your glasses can be protected from the paint, too, if you cover the lenses with plastic wrap.

THE WALLS HAVE YEARS

An electric mixing bowl is super for mixing wallpaper paste. Just be sure to clean immediately before the glue hardens.

Before climbing to the top of the ladder to hang paper, clamp five clothespins to the bottom of the roll so that the bottom edge hangs below the mop board. The paper won't roll up as you're trying to match patterns and there's no chance you'll cut the paper too short.

1880
1930
1949
1976
1999

A sharp razor blade is crucial when cutting wallpaper. To keep it razor sharp and whistle clean, keep it handy in a small bowl with lukewarm water.

When you're applying heavy vinyl wallpaper and can't get the bubbles out, stick a pin into the bubble and smooth. The wall covering will lie flat.

To remove crayon marks from wallpaper:
- Use an ordinary pencil eraser, or
- Dampen a cloth with cool water; add some toothpaste and rub gently. Rinse with a clean damp cloth. Also effective on painted walls.

After wallpapering, save a small amount of paste in a well-marked closed container in the refrigerator. The paste or glue will soften quickly at room temperature and if some of the paper comes loose, you can repaste it before it rips.

RENEW IT AND RE-USE IT

A dirty eraser can be renewed. File it with a nail file or emery board.

An emery board can also be used to tighten tweezers that are too loose. Use the flat edge to file the inside of the tips.

A quick way to sharpen scissors you use for cutting paper: use several thicknesses of aluminum foil or sandpaper and cut through them several times.

A clogged spout or an aerosol can will spray again if you run warm water over it.

To drive a nail without injuring your fingers, hold the nail between the teeth of a comb.

You can prevent your plaster from cracking and falling when you drive a nail into the wall. First put a piece of cellophane tape over the spot where you'll be putting the nail. Only a hole . . . no cracks.

To fasten a screw in plaster when it refuses to hold, pull out the screw, stuff a piece of fine steel wool in the hole, then drive the screw. Voila! It's firmly in place.

If you paint the screw of your drawer knob with fingernail polish before driving it, the screw will hold tightly. No more wobbly knobs!

wax

Do your furniture drawers stick? Remove them and spray the bottom edge and the runners on the furniture with a wax spray, or slide some wet soap over the edges to make the sticky drawers slide easily.

Rain and humidity cause windows to swell and stick. Wash the sides with liquid wax and your windows will open and close with ease. One treatment should last a year.

To temporarily eliminate the annoyance of dripping faucets, tie a string to it and let the string hang down to the drain. Water will run down the string in a stream rather than drops.

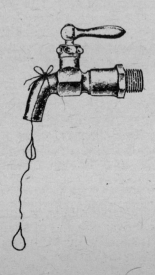

If you have to slam your doors to keep them shut, take a lead pencil and scribble on the inside at the point of the latch and also at the striker. The door should now close with your fingertips.

Hair spray used on hinges unsqueaks creaky doors.

If a pane of window glass cracks and can't be replaced immediately. coat the glass with clear shellac to weatherproof it. This technique used on hairline cracks will prevent them from getting larger. No shellac handy? Use clear nailpolish.

An electric knife is a quick, clean and accurate way of cutting thick foam rubber used for chairs, sofas and pillows.

Renew the appearance of an old box spring by covering with an old fitted sheet. Here's to a brighter and cheerier bedroom!

HERE'S HOW

How to line up your tiebacks: lower a window shade to the proper level and use as a guideline for placement of each curtain tieback.

Cut a finger from an old rubber or cotton glove and place it over one end of a curtain rod . . . makes it easier to insert the rod and prevents catches in the curtain.

Hanging your pictures? Want to find the most attractive arrangement before pounding nails into the wall? Cut cardboard the same dimensions as the pictures. Use a table or floor to move facsimiles around until you decide on desirable positions.

For an extra pair of bookends or for doorstops, cover bricks with felt, contact paper or tape, leftover wrapping paper or fabric material.

RECYCLE FACTORY

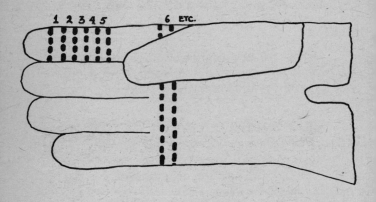

Rather than discard old rubber gloves, cut the fingers widthwise for good small-sized rubber bands and the palm and wrist widthwise for larger bands.

If you pack away an old plastic tablecloth with your Christmas decorations, you'll have a handy drop cloth to put under your tree each year to catch the falling needles.

Make your own pot scrubbers by using empty plastic mesh bags. Cut them open and then into five one-inch strips. Double over and tie in the middle.

Use the same plastic mesh to lengthen the life of your sponges. Cover them with the net which will take the punishment of scrubbing. (Onion bags are a good source.)

Empty cocoa containers can be filled with sand covered with decorative paper or fabric and used as doorstops or bookends.

Turn a useless old 4-legged table into a useless 3-legged table. Use that nice, sturdy leg as a base for a homemade lamp. A coat of varnish or paint will give it a custom look.

Old window shades or plastic place mats can be used for drawer liners. Cut them to size to fit; remove them for easy cleaning.

Use about-to-be-discarded vinyl window shades over a child's mattress as a rubber sheet.

Send out family spies to scout for abandoned telephone cable spools. Depending on size, they make perfect tables given a little paint, paper and imagination.

Plastic rings from six-packs of beverages are potential discards with seemingly magical properties. Link them with twist ties and make the following:
• plant trellis
• volleyball nets
• bird feeders

Flip tops from cans can be used as hangers if attached to the back of a picture or any item you want to hang on the wall with a small nail. They're available and the price is right! (If you're creative and ambitious, flip tops can also be interlocked with each other to make unusual jewelry such as look-again necklaces and pendants.)

There's even a way to recycle empty soda and beer cans. Glue the cans together, 3 high, 3 wide and 7 long. Place a piece of glass or acrylic over the top and you have an inexpensive coffee table that's sure to be a conversation piece. Great for student apartments, family rooms and vacation cottages.

An old metal shower ring makes a sturdy key ring.

Recycle an old lunch box by covering it with contact paper and converting it to a first aid and emergency kit for your car, boat and/or bike bag. Fill it with all your needs for unexpected emergencies from band-aids and aspirin to matches and scissors.

Use an old TV tray stand for a plastic trash bag holder. Open up the stand, slip the bag in and overlap each side about 10 inches. You now have an extra trash barrel for workshop, basement, kitchen or for after a cookout for quick clean-ups.

PAPER POWER

A good source for free paper plates is the sturdy, colorful trays the supermarket uses to pack its produce and meat. They're great for picnics or home use.

Turn junk mail into useful paper. Save clean-on-one-side pieces of paper to write for TV offers, order merchandise and magazines, etc. Except for formal or personal correspondence, the recipient couldn't care less what you write on--only what you write!

Old shoe boxes can be covered in decorative paper and used for holding small toys in a child's room, sauce and salad dressing mixes in the kitchen, odds 'n ends in the bathroom and stationery needs on a desk. They can also be used for a file box for 5 x 8 cards.

Wax paper wrappers from bread are excellent for wrapping lunch bag food. And don't forget to reuse your cereal and cracker box liners. You can use them wherever you need wax paper. They're particularly handy for storing refrigerator cookies.

Bread bags and the twist ties that come with them make convenient garbage disposal bags.

Things to do with leftover rolls of wallpaper, store discards and wallpaper sample books:
- scrapbooks for children's drawings and stories
- mat for pictures
- gift wrapping paper
- book covers
- decorative covering for cigar boxes (makes attractive jewelry boxes)
- coordinate material for room accessories, such as wastebaskets and lampshades.

BOTTLED UP!

Place empty perfume bottles in lingerie drawers. They'll provide a pleasant scent for an extended time.

Two recipes for a stamp or letter moistener:

1) an old shampoo bottle filled with water
   and a small piece of sponge stuffed
   into the opening of the bottle;

2) a nearly empty rubber-tipped mucilage
   bottle. Fill with water and shake.
No more "yucky" taste when you're
preparing your letters for mailing.

Soda and wine bottles turn into handsome
ceramic-looking vases when small pieces of
masking tape — torn randomly from the roll
— are first applied over the entire surface of
the bottle and then coated with brown shoe
polish. The edges of the tape absorb most of
the polish and give drab bottles an authentic
and expensive look.

To remove a cork that fell into a bottle you
want to recycle, pour just enough ammonia in
the empty bottle to float the cork. Let it
stand at least 24 hours. The ammonia will
erode the cork so it will crumble.

Empty clean plastic dish detergent bottles
have a number of secondary uses including
dispensing barbecue sauce as needed,
applying setting lotion, or watering plants.

Recycle a leaking hot water bottle by filling it with sand and using as a kneeling pad. Prevents housemaid's or gardener's knee.

FRIENDLY FIRES

Empty milk cartons are great for kindling rip-roaring fires! Save them for evenings by the fire or sunny Sunday barbecues in open-fire pits.

Recycle charcoal after barbecuing by first lining the grill with aluminum foil. After use, seal the aluminum foil liner around the hot coals. The coals will go out, but some of them will remain usable for the next barbecue.

You don't have to dowse your charcoal with gasoline to start your backyard barbecue burning brightly. Just fill each compartment of an empty cardboard egg container with a charcoal briquette. Close the container and put it on top of the coals in the grille. Set the carton afire and the rest of the coals will soon be burning nicely.

Dried citrus rinds are terrific, aromatic kindling for fires.

Chapter 10
STITCH-N-TIME
sewing and other needle arts

PINS 'N NEEDLES

A safety razor is an excellent tool for ripping seams. But keep it from ripping anything else by placing it inside a small metal or plastic pill container inside your sewing box or machine.

Also keep a soap end in your sewing box to use as a tailor's chalk. It washes out easily.

After letting down hems, remove the lines left on the garment by rubbing vinegar on the crease. Press with a warm iron. The white lines on denim can be removed with a blue crayon.

Cover a plain steel wool pad with colorful fabric. Lo and behold — a pin cushion!

Thread will stay untangled if the ends are taped to the spool. No more hunting and poking for the end of the thread.

Polyester thread is tricky and tends to twist, but if you rub it on a bar of soap or beeswax before use, you'll prevent this annoyance.

To thread a yarn needle quickly and easily, cut a piece of paper which, when folded, is somewhat less than the width and length of the needle's eye. Insert the yarn in the paper which will pass easily through the eye of the needle. A small piece of tape (cut to size) on one end of the yarn will also do the trick. The tape will just peel off so no yarn is lost.

If you have difficulty in threading needles because of sight or nerve problems, have someone else thread several different needles on to various spools for you. Whenever anyone visits, have them re-thread any you've used in the interim.

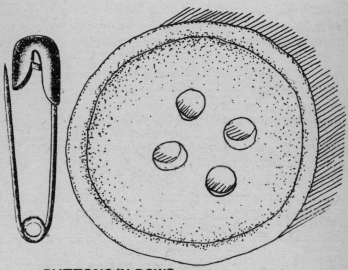

BUTTONS 'N BOWS

Matching buttons will stay together in your sewing box if you thread a needle and pass it through one hole of each button or string them all on a safety pin. This should be done when cutting buttons from a discarded garment so that they are all pre-sorted and easy to count when needed.

Use dental floss or fishing line to sew buttons. Both are exceptionally strong and especially good for any children's clothing that gets rough wear.

A dab of colorless nail polish on the center of
each button on your clothes seals the thread
and minimizes the nuisance of constantly
sewing on buttons.

Four-hole buttons will stay attached longer
if you sew through only two holes at a time.
Break the thread and knot it for each set of
holes. If one thread gives way, the other
will hold. If sewn diagonally, when one set
breaks, the tension will remain more evenly
distributed and the buttons won't be
"flop-sided."

When sewing on snap fasteners, sew all the
snaps on one side first. Put chalk over them
and press against the opposite side. This marks
the correct place for attaching the other half
of the fasteners and assures a correct fit.

If your snap is popping, give the side of the
snap a tap with a hammer. It will spread just
enough to fit snugly into the hollow half of
the snap.

PATTERN PATTER

Make your own patterns by taking an existing item you like and tracing around it onto a newspaper. Leave enough space for seam allowances and darts. Cut it out and use as a regular pattern.

A good substitute for a pattern tracer when sewing is a pizza cutter. We're not so sure we'd recommend the reverse though!

Instead of using pins to fasten material to a pattern, try cellophane tape. The pattern lies flat and you can cut right through the tape.

Store sewing patterns you want to save rolled up inside paper toweling and wrapping paper tubes. Label each so they're easy to identify when needed. (Same type of tubes can also be used for storing leftover fabric.)

Put your re-usable patterns in a large manila envelope. Paste the pattern picture and the fabric requirements from the original envelope on the front.

Decorate laundry bags, toy bags or other items items with iron-on patches cut in the shape of letters, numerals or animals. Make your own or use a store-bought stencil if you want special iron-on designs.

When making quilts, cut patterns from medium sandpaper. They will cling to the cloth. If the patches are too large, use table oil cloth which can easily be pinned to the material over and over without tearing.

TREADLES OR PEDALS

Keep a plastic straw in or near your sewing machine for when you are re-filling or changing the bobbin. That's the time to blow the lint away from the internal machinery.

When filling your sewing machine bobbin, just put a small amount of contrasting thread on the beginning of the bobbin. Knot it to the color thread you are going to use; then fill the bobbin as usual. When you're sewing, the contrasting thread will serve as a warning that your bobbin has run out and it's time to refill.

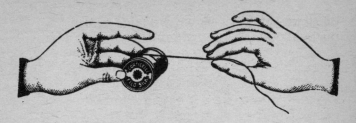

Tape a small bag onto your sewing machine to put threads in as clipped. Saves cleaning up afterwards. (See "Mother Earth's Offspring" for what to do with the bag when it's nearly filled!)

To prevent your electric sewing machine pedal from sliding on the floor, put an "octopus" soap holder under it. If slightly dampened first, this plastic disc with rows of suction cups on both sides will stick to both the floor and the foot pedal.

SECOND TIME AROUND

Make attractive tablecloths and napkins from muslin sheets bought at discount stores. To cover round tables, cut out a circle and use pinking shears to eliminate the need to hem. The same material can also be used for window treatments and other room decorations. Square-yard prices for sheets are much cheaper than material bought off the bolt. And the width of the sheets allows for seamless cloth.

When you purchase new flat sheets, rip out
the small hem and sew a large hem in its place
to match the top exactly. Now when you
make the bed the sheet can face either way.
The wear will be more evenly distributed
which will prolong the sheet's usefulness.

To revive the life of worn-out sheets, rip them
down the center. Seam the selvedge (outside
edges) together. Now the center, where the
strength is needed, is sturdy.

There's enough material in one old sheet for
it to be recycled into three new pillow cases.

For blankets that are too short for the bed,
sew a strip of muslin to the end of the
blanket. Keep it tucked under the mattress.

One washcloth — cut diagonally — can make two baby bibs. Sew a ribbon across the cut edges to serve as ties and to give the bibs a finished look.

To make a quick apron, use a hand or kitchen towel. Sew a hem on one end and insert elastic. Adjust to the right size and pin.

No more hunting for potholders when you need them. If you sew potholders to the lower corners of an apron, they'll always be available at the right moment.

Fine Draperies

Don't struggle over mending tears in thin material such as curtains. Place a piece of tissue paper over the hole and stitch over it. The paper comes off when the curtain is laundered and the tear will be patched as perfectly and invisibly as possible.

To rid garments of tiny holes left by ripping out a seam, moisten a cloth with vinegar, place under the holes and press with a hot iron.

When mending socks, turn them inside out, put a light bulb inside and darn. The bulb gives you the shape you need at the heel or toe.

Polo shirts that have frayed cuffs or have become too small can be altered into tank tops. Scoop the neckline, remove the sleeves, turn the edges and hem.

When running a new elastic or tape through pajamas or pants, pin an end of the old and new together. As the old is pulled out, the new elastic or tape will be pulled through.

Before discarding an old full slip, consider cutting and hemming it just below the waist. Now you have a camisole to wear under see-through blouses.

Save old panty hose. Cut off the waistband and save for sewing projects requiring elastic waistbands. The hose part can be used for stuffing toys and pillows.

Before discarding a fake fur coat, take another look. It might make a cute area rug for a child's room if cut into a geometric or animal shape.

MATCHING IT UP

Close cover before shopping! Empty matchbooks are neat carriers for swatches of fabric or thread you want to match. Just tape the swatch or thread to the inside and close.

Make customized earrings from attractive buttons. Use ear wires for pierced ears and slip through the holes of the buttons. A dot of glue helps to keep them in place.

Wash your knitting needles before using and the yarn will slide along the needles very smoothly.

If the tip of a bone knitting needle breaks, it can be made serviceable again by sharpening in a pencil sharpener.

Keep scraps of yarn to crochet colorful doilies and rugs. Tie the scraps together to make longer lengths. Use a size 10 or T crochet hook.

Transform a single sock from a half-lost pair into a doll's outfit. The stretchiness in the sock will allow it to fit a variety of dolls. If the mate turns up when it's too late — well, there's always another doll to be outfitted!

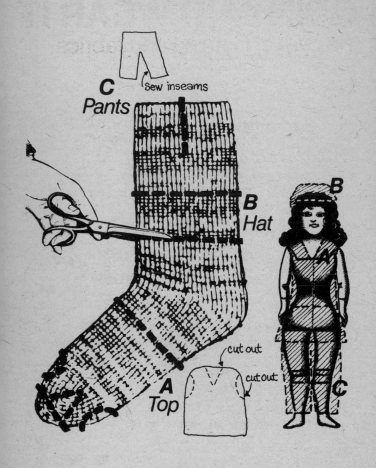

C
Pants

sew inseams

B
Hat

B

A
Top

cut out

cut out

C

Chapter 11
GRIN AND WEAR IT
the care of clothing and fabrics

THAT'S SHOE BIZ

Are mothballs an effective shoe deodorant? Shoe-er! You'll keep shoes and boots fresh if you tie a few mothballs in a cheesecloth or any leftover fabric and keep them inside the shoes while you're not wearing them.

To clean white shoes and bags, use a small amount of rubbing alcohol or nail polish remover on a cotton ball and rub to remove scuff marks. No need for messy white shoe polish.

But if you must use white shoe polish to clean shoes, spray them with hair spray after cleaning and the polish won't rub off.

Another substitute for shoe polish is spray furniture wax. Just spray and wipe. It's good for all types of shoes.

Renew patent leather shoes, bags and belts by rubbing with petroleum jelly on a soft cloth. Bring to a shine with a clean dry cloth or paper towel.

An easy way to shine shoes is to use a toothbrush rather than a rag. It gets into all the designs and cracks.

To keep suede shoes looking fresh, rub with a piece of stale bread or rubber sponge after each wearing.

Prolong the life of children's sneakers that have worn through the canvas, by using iron-on tape patches cut into decorative shapes. Your child will have a unique, fun pair of sneakers.

Place paper towel tubes inside tall boots to keep them standing tall!

STALKING STOCKINGS

Keep nylon hose long lasting by putting on a pair of peds before pulling on your panty hose. Toenails and rough heels will no longer be run-ners.

Another hint for preserving nylons: dissolve one teaspoon of gelatin in a pint of hot water. Let the water cool, then rinse the nylons in it.

Colorless nail polish dabbed on the run of a stocking will keep it from running further and will hold during a wash.

SWEATER OR KNOT

If your sweater has more pills than a pharmacy, then shave away your sweater stubble! Extend the life and attractiveness of a favorite sweater by laying the sweater out flat and going over the pilled area with an electric razor. No harm to the razor; spruces up the sweater.

If you don't have an electric razor, you can still remove those tiny knots or wool balls on your sweaters or slacks by sandpapering them. Use fine sandpaper and rub gently. Clothes get months or years of extra wear.

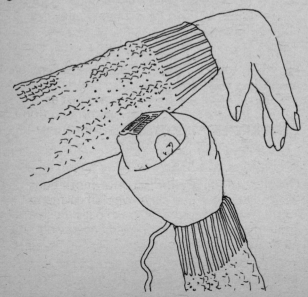

Table napkins are much cheaper than head scarves so buy the under $1.00 ones that are 18" x 18" and use as a peasant scarf around the neck.

Stays never seem to stay around. Make your own extra stays for shirt collars. Before they get lost, take a metal stay, trace around it on a plastic bottle and cut out with utility scissors. Keep handy for dressing time.

THE MOTHBALL FEAT

To remove dust and lint from clothing, use a dry or mildly damp sponge and rub gently.

Old pillowcases make excellent dust covers for clothing. Simply cut a tiny hole in the seamed end and slip over the hanger hook and clothes.

To mothball or not to mothball. . . . Save soap ends to place among woolens during the summer. They provide a more pleasant odor than moth balls or flakes and are just as effective. At the end of the season you don't have to air them to remove the lingering, unpleasant moth ball odor.

You can eliminate the need for moth balls entirely by hanging *clean* woolen garments inside large green plastic trash bags. Push a hole through the top for the hangers and tape the opening at the bottom.

DON'T FAIL TO GIVE SIZE

STAIN STRAIN

Stains from the grass? Alas! Now you can remove them by first washing the stain in alcohol and rinsing in clear water. If at all possible, attack the stain while it's still fresh.

Among the many uses for hair spray . . . stain removal. It works on most fabrics and is effective in removing grease, fruit stains and ball point pen marks. Spray, rub and if necessary repeat.

Ink can also be removed by soaking the stained garment in milk. If the stain is dry, use sour salt, first wetting the spot then rubbing the salts on and rinsing well with cold water. It is sometimes necessary to repeat the procedure but the ink will eventually disappear.

Another ink stain remover is rubbing alcohol. It makes the ink spots disappear quickly.

On leather use toothpaste as an ink stain remover.

To remove cooking oil:

1) Sprinkle talcum powder on the stain as soon as possible.
2) Leave on for 5-7 minutes.
3) Brush off. Stain will have been absorbed by the powder.

or

1) Saturate the spot with cooking oil and rub into the soiled area.
2) Put washing powder over the oil and let stand for a few minutes.
3) Put in lukewarm water and wash.

or

1) Make a paste of dry detergent and cold water.
2) Rub the paste into the stain. (The fabric must be dry.)
3) Rinse in cold water.

Especially effective for permanent press clothing.

To remove clay, play putty or gum from clothing, place in the freezer for several hours. Scrape gently with a serrated knife. Then remove the thin gummy layer left on by rinsing in hot water. An ice cube applied to the gummed-up area will work the same way.

Wax may be removed from fabric by placing a piece of paper towel or brown bag over and under the stain and ironing over the spot. The paper will absorb the melted wax. Keep moving the stained paper so as not to soil unspotted areas.

If someone has spilled wine on the tablecloth at a gay and festive occasion, carry off the situation with aplomb. Rub a generous amount of salt into the spot. The salt will absorb the wine. When the cloth is washed, both salt and stain will disappear.

To remove spots created by any alcoholic drinks, sponge them with water, pour on a liquid detergent and rub between the hands. Let stand for a half hour and then rinse thoroughly. Wash as usual.

Plain, unadulterated tea (no sugar, no milk, no lemon, please!) will remove stains from dark fabrics without leaving a stain of its own.

Another beverage to use as an emergency stain remover is soda or sparkling water. Sponge thoroughly.

To remove berry stains from washable fabrics, hold the stained fabric taut and pour boiling water through the stain. Like magic, you'll be able to watch it disappear.

HAND-SOMELY CLEAN

A silly but hand-saving way to wash laundry by hand is to use a short-handled sink plunger! Using a heated pick or nail to puncture the rubber, make several air holes in the suction cup to allow water to circulate.

When handwashing a piece of clothing that has both dark and white colors, add a couple of pinches of salt to the soapy water. It will help keep the dark colors from running.

How to wash leather gloves: wear the gloves while washing them. Use a shampoo or soap with lanolin to restore the oil to the glove skins. A few drops of olive oil added to the rinse will keep doeskin, pigskin and chamois gloves soft and pliant. Roll gloves off your hands after washing since pulling stretches the glove fingers out of shape. Washable leather gloves will dry softer after washing if they are rolled for a minute in a moist terry towel. Push a clothespin (old fashioned type) carefully into the fingers of the newly washed gloves to keep them from losing shape while drying.

A few drops of leftover or unwanted cologne
or toilet water in the rinse water when
washing hosiery or lingerie will impart a
pleasant, lingering odor to your intimate
apparel.

Let the driving do the washing! When on a driving vacation, put soiled clothes, hot water and detergent in a plastic container. Close securely, put in the car trunk and forget. By the time you reach your evening's destination, your clothes will be washed and need only be rinsed and hung to dry.

To wash feather pillows, place them in the bath and rub with shampoo and water. Then jog on them. Result: clean pillows and good exercise.

PREWASH PRE-THINK

For ring-around-the-collar keep a bottle of shampoo near your laundry supplies. Swish shampoo around wet collars, rub in and then throw into the regular wash.

Cottons can be whitened by soaking them in a mixture of dishwasher detergent, a little bleach and hot water before they're tossed into the washing machine.

When using liquid detergent, measure in a cup the amount needed for a wash. Use a clean paint or pastry brush to apply the solution right on to the stain. It's less wasteful than pouring directly from a large container.

Despite box directions on laundry detergent, use only about a quarter of a cup of detergent for each normal laundry load—up to 18 pounds. Smaller amounts of detergent do the job and reduce residue on the clothes, clogged washing machines and water pollution. Water conditioners and pre-treatment of stains usually eliminate the need for bleach.

Don't drag detergent! Those who use laundry-rooms and laundromats away from home should pre-measure soap powders and pour the proper amount into a white sock for light washes and a dark sock for dark washes. Empty directly into machines and keep those big, economy-size boxes at home!

Place a pin cushion with medium-sized pins near the clothes hamper or laundry bag and get all family members in the habit of pinning their socks together before tossing them in the hamper. Keeps socks together with their mates. No more pairing woes at the end of wash day.

MACHINE MAGIC

Use cold water when washing almost everything except extremely soiled clothing. It saves on your hot water bill and there will be no discernible difference in the results.

When washing woolen blankets or quilts made of wool scraps, add one cup of mothballs or crystals to the rinse water. The blankets will be protected from moths for the season.

Bleach substitute: two capfuls of white vinegar added to the wash and one capful added to the rinse water.

If you've put too much detergent in a washing machine, and it's getting sudsy, the addition of some fabric softener or a small piece of hand soap will cut the suds.

When your washing machine agitator gets stiff and squeaks, pull it off and add a small amount of petroleum jelly around the top of the pipe. Remove soap and dirt that has accumulated around the pipe. Don't worry, no grease will get on the clothes.

When doing a load of wash in a machine, gather all dirty combs, put them into an old sock and knot the end. Let the combs run through the wash cycle. Remove and rinse in hot water!

And to keep dark socks from picking up lint in a washer or dryer, place them in an old nylon stocking and tie the end loosely before laundering.

DRYING-OUT

If you're hanging your clothes on an outdoor line during the winter, add one tablespoon of salt to the rinse water to prevent them from freezing.

Your clothespins won't split or freeze either if you boil them in a strong salt solution.

And if you keep your clothespins outdoors attached to the clothes line, use a net bag that a turkey comes in as a container. When it rains, the water won't collect in the bag.

A clothespin holder can also be made from a large empty bleach bottle. Cut a front top opening large enough so your hand goes in and out freely. Leave the handle on to attach to the line and punch a couple of small holes in the bottom for drainage of excess water.

When putting slacks out to dry, turn the pockets inside out and use the pockets to attach the slacks to the line. No more clothespin marks on the legs.

If you're hanging a coat or a dress on the line, use two coat hangers, hooked in opposite directions to prevent the wind from blowing the garment off the line.

Remove lint and fluff up decorator pillows by putting them into a dryer at a cool setting.

GOING TO PRESS

Regular liquid starch in a plastic spray bottle is less expensive than buying spray starch in an aerosol can.

To make shirt ironing easier, after sprinkling clothes put them in the freezer for a half-hour. The iron will glide over the wrinkles smoothly and quickly.

If you run out of time to complete your ironing after sprinkling your clothes, place the items in the refrigerator overnight. They'll stay damp for the next day.

or

Keep your dampened clothes in a plastic bag to prevent evaporation. You won't waste time repeating the sprinkling.

If you add a few drops of cologne before putting water in a steam iron, clothes will have a pleasant smell. And it doesn't hurt the iron.

Declogging a steam iron: fill the water chamber with white vinegar and let it stand overnight. Rinse several times to remove all the vinegar.

A sheet of heavy duty aluminum foil placed between an ironing board pad and cover helps use heat from the iron more efficiently by reflecting heat back to the material being ironed. The foil also prevents steam from dampening the pad. Especially effective for iron-on patches.

To get a nice sharp crease in a pair of slacks, press with a damp cloth. Immediately before the steam escapes press again with a dry newspaper. For lighter colors use a brown paper bag.

Small, flat ribbons can be ironed by quickly
running them over a turned on clean light
bulb. But don't use a bulb that has been on
for a long time. It may be too hot and the
ribbons will catch fire.

One cup of epsom salts in the rinse water will
make it easy to iron items like ruffled
curtains. They come out wrinkleless and
rejuvenated.

But don't bother to iron fiberglass draperies.
Hang them up as they come out of the washer
and shape them the way you want them to
hang. Very little moisture is left after machine
washing and they will dry right in place.

No need to iron linen handkerchiefs or small
linen napkins. Just smooth them when wet on
a mirror, refrigerator door or bathtub. When

dry, they look as though a professional
had ironed them.

After washing a lace tablecloth or curtain,
place on a table covered with a plastic cloth.
Stretch the tablecloth or curtain on the
plastic and press with your hands. After it's
dry, just a light touch up with an iron is all
that's necessary.

Do your permanent press wearables need a
little touch-up? Fold them on their creases
and SIT ON THEM! Saves all kinds of time
and energy.

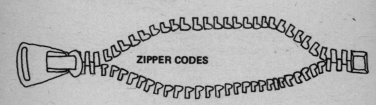

ZIPPER CODES

Zippers can be made less vulnerable to breaks
if they are always closed before a garment is
placed in a wash. After they dry, put a drop
of 3-in-1 oil on them. (Don't drip on clean
fabric.) It will smooth the track and lengthen
their life.

But when zippers no longer go up and down
with ease, zip them all the way up. Then rub
the zipper teeth with the point of a pencil in
an up and down motion. The graphite of the
pencil lead lubricates the zipper track. A piece
of paraffin will do the same trick.

Chapter 12
GETTING IT ALL TOGETHER
think-ahead thoughts

SYSTEMS AND CATEGORIES

Color code your keys and locks for easy
identification. A spot of the same color paint
on matching key and lock will put an end to
hopeless gropings. Instant open!

Keep a cassette tape player near your TV to
record recipes or other information you want
for future references for either yourself or
someone who was not able to be there at
broadcast time.

Record albums will stand when one is
removed from a shelf if a sheet of corrugated
cardboard is placed in the back of the cabinet.
The ridges keep the remaining albums upright.

Large empty detergent boxes make good
storage units for knitting or travel books as
well as periodicals you may wish to save. Cut
off the top of a large box; cut diagonally

across both wide sides of the box to about
1/2 the length of the narrow side of the box.
Cover with decorative adhesive paper,
recycled wallpaper or leftover fabric.

Use a recipe box for addresses rather than a
book. It's easier to replace a card with a new
address than scratch out an old address and
write in a new one.

If you prefer to keep an address book, write
only the name in ink and the address and
phone number in pencil. A good eraser will
allow you to keep an updated, easy-to-read
list.

SHOPPING HOPPING

Make your shopping list your road map.
Before shopping not only make a list of items
but put them in the sequence of your route of
stores and aisles in your supermarket.
Then you can zip up and down the aisles of
the supermarket and go to the next store
without retracing steps.

When grocery shopping on hot days, take an insulated picnic bag with you. It'll keep perishables fresh.

Watch for all expiration dates on food items. If items are on sale because the expiration date is close, be sure you can use those items shortly after purchase.

So as not to forget to hand in your eligible coupons when checking out, write "coupon" next to the item on your shopping list.

Clip all the money-saving coupons of your favorite market. When shopping, drop the coupon for items you do not wish to buy alongside the market's display. Then a shopper who does want the product can pick up the coupon and use it. Some supermarkets even have a box of excess coupons for swapping purposes. You'll find them at the courtesy desk. Recycle coupons!

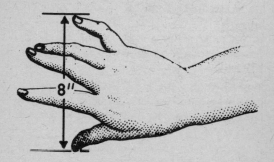

8"

Memorize the length of the span of your hand from the top of your thumb and the tip of your little finger. It's a do-it-yourself tape measure that will come in handy when you're shopping and want to see if an item is the right size.

$6\frac{1}{8}$"

You can also use a dollar bill as an "instant measuring stick." It's 6-1/8 inches long; figure from there.

CLOSET CLUTTER

How frustrating when you are preparing to dress to find the clothes you intended to wear have fallen off the hanger onto the closet floor and need to be ironed. To prevent recurrence, wrap a rubber band near each end of a coat hanger and garments won't slip off.

If your clothes closet pole is wooden, make notches at regular intervals. Your clothes will organize themselves. No more bunching up in one spot!

Not enough room in your closet to accommodate all those skirts and slacks? Attach a towel rack to the inside of the door and hang skirts and slacks over the bar.

Cut a small window in a shoe box and tape plastic wrap over the hole so you can see through and easily identify what you've stored there.

Use a pocket shoe organizer in or near the closet for all those mittens, gloves and scarves.

To dry mittens, gloves, and scarves quickly over a floor heater, nail 6 clothespins to a foot-long board on the wall above the register. Just clip the mittens and let them blow dry.

LET THERE BE LIGHT

Eliminate the annoyance of pulling the wrong cord to let in the light by putting a dot of red nail polish on the pull that opens the venetian blinds or drapes.

If your lighter uses flints, store an extra flint under the cotton pad in the underside of the lighter mechanism. It'll be there when you need it. Be sure to put another one in for the next replacement as soon as possible.

You can shorten your lamp cord without cutting it by wrapping it tightly around a broom handle and letting it stay overnight. Like your telephone wire, the cord will stay spiraled and short.

TIS BETTER TO GIFT

Whenever you get your calendar for the upcoming year, make a notation on the date you should mail a card or gift for any occasion. Many events are missed because they're not noticed until the day arrives or is past.

If you find a card that would be appropriate for a specific person, even though it may be months in advance, purchase it. Write the date to mail it in the upper right hand corner where it will eventually be covered by a stamp. (But do get into the habit of checking the card again before it's mailed to make sure it's still apropos.)

When giving birthday or other greeting cards in person leave the envelope blank and unsealed. The recipient will have your message plus an extra envelope as a bonus!

Keep sales slips from all gift purchases. Write the recipient on the back. In case returns are necessary, the slip is easily retrievable.

Make gift wrap paper for small items by saving the colorful bags in which card, gift and department stores place your purchases. Cut away portions with any printing and store the usable sections until needed.

Gifts for children can be wrapped in the colorful comic sections from the Sunday papers, kitchen gifts in supermarket ads, sports gifts in the sports section, gifts for investor in the stock listings, etc. A cheery ribbon makes the recycled wrap look attractive.

Wrap the gift for a Silver Anniversary in aluminum foil.

A going-away present wrapped in a road map of the recipient's destination will be appreciated.

Decorate a birthday gift with a picture of the recipient — preferably one of years before and long forgotten. You can't roll back the years but you can bring back the memories.

Use something other than paper occasionally for gift wrapping. For example: for a bridal shower, wrap the items in kitchen towels with a wooden spoon; for baby showers, wrap in a diaper and decorate with a rattle. The bonus gifts will be remembered and used, too.

For wedding showers decorate a card file box and include a collection of your own favorite recipes. You'll be giving the bride your own personal cookbook.

When wrapping gifts for small children don't tape the edges tightly and avoid frustrating small, anxious hands.

For a favor for children's parties attach names to candy bars and use them as place cards.

Another child's party favor idea is a little
more time-consuming but cheaper and more
creative than buying favors. Fill empty toilet
paper rolls with candy and tiny toys. Cover
with pretty paper, put each child's name on it
and use as both a place card and a take-home
favor.

Take photos of each child attending your
child's birthday party and use the back of the
picture for a thank you note for the birthday
gift. This idea can be used for adult occasions
as well. One picture is worth a thousand
words.

For crispy dollar bills to give away as gifts —
spray with starch and iron!

Whenever you send a hand-made (sewn,
knitted, crocheted) item to a friend as a gift,
remember to enclose the laundering
instructions.

Use cardboard tubes to hold small gifts.
Makes them easier to wrap and easier to pack
for mailing.

POSTAL SECURITY

When stamps are stuck together, place in the
freezer for about an hour. They can be
separated with the glue still intact.

Place items to be mailed in a plastic bag with
the complete address and return address.
Then wrap with paper. In case of bad weather

or damage to the wrapping, item is safe and identifiable and will still probably reach its destination.

To make a string holder use a pretty teapot and lead the string through the spout.

Tie tight, secure packages with wet string. It shrinks as it dries and gets tighter.

To secure each knot so it will not untie, dab each end of the string with natural nail polish.

Old patterns and nylon stockings can be used to wrap around breakable items. They're light weight and absorb shock. Whether you're moving lots of household items or just mailing one item, they make good packing material.

If the item you're mailing is fragile, place
inside a plastic bag and then inflate as you
would a balloon. The air pocket helps prevent
breakage.

MOVE EASY

Prepare your moving notices to friends and
family well in advance of your moving date.
Then they'll be ready for mailing when you
arrive at your new address.

Packing to move? If you need lots of cord, cut old nylon hose crosswise. The strips make extra strong string for boxes.

Save men's old socks for wrapping around shoes when packing.

When doing your own packing for a move, use different color masking tape as a code to denote the rooms where the boxes are to go. Makes unloading much more efficient.

A box of essentials for immediate use upon arriving at your new home will make moving less of a trauma. Include linens, cleaning paraphernalia, soap, light bulbs, paper cups and even snacks. Label "last in, first out."

Chapter 13
THE LIVING END
an offbeat assortment of ideas

PEANUTS — IN A NUTSHELL! (242, $2.95)
by Jeffrey Feinman

Believe it or not, a complete guide to a most unusual — though amazingly versatile — cooking ingredient: The Peanut! Have you heard of SLAW CACHUETTE? ... of PEANUT STUFFED SQUASH? ... of PEANUT BAKED FLOUNDER? ... If you haven't, then it's about time you made the most palatable encounter of your life!

THE TWO ASSASSINS (214, $1.95)
by Dr. Renatus Hartogs and Lucy Freeman

OSWALD and RUBY — who were they? What made them tick? Why did each, in his own way, commit a history-changing murder? A prominent psychiatrist and a well-known author analyze the Warren Report, examine testimony of countless witnesses, and explain the minds of these two assassins.

APPOINTMENT IN DALLAS (100, $1.95)
by Hugh McDonald

An incredible story of the man who refused to believe that the Dallas Police Department had the true assassin of President Kennedy in Lee Harvey Oswald. With over 40 years experience in police and intelligence work, Hugh McDonald covered 50,000 miles and spent a number of years looking for "Saul," the professional killer who pulled the trigger on JFK. You can read "Saul's" COMPLETE CONFESSION in this book!

Available wherever paperbacks are sold, or order direct from the Publisher. Send cover price plus 25¢ per copy for mailing and handling to ZEBRA BOOKS, 521 Fifth Avenue, New York, NY 10017. DO NOT SEND CASH!